THE WORLD OF SALT SHAKERS

By

Mildred and Ralph Lechner

COLLECTOR BOOKS
P.O. Box 3009
Paducah, KY 42001

The current values in this book should be used only as a guide. They are not intended to set prices, which vary from one section of the country to another. Auction prices as well as dealer prices vary greatly and are affected by condition as well as demand. Neither the Author nor the Publisher assumes responsibility for any losses that might be incurred as a result of consulting this guide.

Additional copies of this book may be ordered from:

COLLECTOR BOOKS
P.O. Box 3009
Paducah, Kentucky 42001

or

The Authors, Mr. and Mrs. Ralph Lechner
P.O. Box 554
Mechanicsville, VA 23111

@ $9.95 Add $1.00 for postage and handling.

Printed by IMAGE GRAPHICS, Paducah, Kentucky

INDEX & SECTION LISTING

SECTION I

SECTION II

Alphabetical Listing By Manufacturer's Name

SECTION III

POTPOURRI INDEX

* * * * * * * *

WE DEDICATE THIS BOOK

TO

OUR DAUGHTERS

GENEVIEVE, BEVERLY AND ELLEN

SPECIAL ACKNOWLEDGEMENT

Margaret and Douglas Archer of Ballwin, Missouri, antique dealers and authors of "Glass Candlesticks", contributed many hours of consultation and coordination to make this book possible. As close personal friends, Margaret and Doug collected side by side with us for a number of years. It is primarily as a result of their personal interest that our book has reached a publisher. The final arrangement and content of this book are the direct result of their assistance in organizing hundreds of pages of our research material; much of which was far too detailed to be included in a book that is designed to provide collectors with quick-look, decisive type, information. For such unselfish, time consuming effort, we shall be eternally grateful.

Mildred & Ralph Lechner

ACKNOWLEDGMENTS TO AUTHORS

We would like to take this opportunity to thank two Authors for their kind consideration in allowing us to reference their publications. They have established many of the pattern names that identify the salt shakers in our publication.

WE THANK YOU:

AUTHUR G. PETERSON
DeBary, Florida

"Glass Salt Shakers: 1000 Patterns" - Published in 1970
"Glass Patents and Patterns" - Published in 1973

EDWIN G. WARMAN
Uniontown, Pennsylvania

"Milk Glass Addenda" - Third Edition, - Published in 1966

ACKNOWLEDGMENTS

We wish to express our gratitude and appreciation to the following individuals who have, in one way or another, contributed their time, consultation and support to this book.

Victor W. Buck,
Upland, Calif . . . . .One of the leading authorities on Art & pattern glass in the West, Victor enriched our lives with his personal friendship, technical advice and guidance, as well as the gift of several shakers to our collection over the years.

Bennie Lawson,
San Luis Obispo,
Calif . . . . .For his encouragement, and the gift of several rare salt shakers to our collection.

Mary Buck,
Upland, Calif . . . . .A very knowledgable antique dealer and personal friend. Her many contributions are a principal factor in the writing of this book.

Vince and Vi Baffa,
Santa Monica, Calif . . . . .For their personal support, consultation and especially their friendship.

B. Bernard Ratzman,
Belvidere, N.J. . . . ."Bernie", as we call him, contributed his personal consultation, support and friendship.

Tillie Ratzman,
Belvidere, N.J. . . . . .For her friendship and assistance in typing the final manuscript.

Don and Marguerite Wolf,
Belvidere, N.J. . . . . .For their friendship and access to their collection of Early American Pattern Glass for study & research.

Jeannine Printz,
Westminister, Calif. . . . . .Who devoted many hours to typing our research material.

Wilma A. Shouse,
Kernersville, N.C. . . . . .For her editorial expertise in correcting many of our grammatical errors.

Miss Nancy Harding
and her staff, Belvidere,
New Jersey. . . . . .Who took that extra time to acquire the many documents we required to finalize the details of writing this book. Our hats are off to the Warren County Library.

Finally, we extend our special thanks to all those individuals at the various museums, libraries and glass houses that we have visited over the last two decades, who assisted us in our research.

INTRODUCTION

In writing this book, it has been our principal objective to only document information that will be useful to collectors of art and pattern glass. It is significant to note that salt shakers were produced in the majority of all glass patterns.

Having spent more than two decades at collecting, we have had a liberal education relative to the pitfalls that may be encountered along the various antiquing trails.

As a result, we are certain that identification ranks high in priority among the information that is most needed by all collectors. The data presented in this publication is, we believe, identification oriented.

To achieve satisfactory results, all the patterns had to be clearly illustrated. Credit must be given to our foresighted Publisher, Bill Schroeder, for producing a quality book through the magic of modern color photography. This, coupled with the talents of our photographer, Bruce Linker, provides the necessary clarity needed for individual pattern identification.

To further accomplish our goal, the reader will find that the various colors listed for each piece are based primarily upon our own personal observations, rather than reported information. This conservative approach may not be complete, but it does eliminate errors. Most of all, collectors will not be searching for a color that does not exist. Our experience has concluded that just because a manufacturing glass house produced a particular color in a bowl, dish, cruet etc. of a particular pattern, does not necessarily mean it is to be found in salt and pepper shakers.

Finally, we have included manufacturer attribution, the approximate age of each item, and have identified (by the abbreviation NA) those patterns that have been Named by the Authors.

We suggest that you take the time to read all the information presented, and make good use of our cross indexing. We believe that you will be provided with considerable assistance in making the various decisions associated with collecting.

Mildred & Ralph Lechner

A SUGGESTED METHOD OF COLLECTING SALT SHAKERS

The salt shakers presented in this book are taken from our private collection. This means that caution was exercised, since our own money was involved, prior to each purchase. To get the most personal satisfaction as collectors, we expended considerable effort to acquire each piece at a reasonable price so that its market value was worth more, at the time of purchase, than we paid for it.

The only way to accomplish this, without haggling, was through constant study and research. It was often quite surprising how little attention was paid to the value of the lowly salt shaker by antique dealers, despite the fact that this ware was manufactured as an integral part of practically every grouping of pattern, cut and art glass produced by American glass houses.

The value of individual knowledge becomes even more important today, because the collector is unfortunately faced with a never-ending flow of reproductions. Already, too many old patterns have essentially become too risky to collect.

ATTRIBUTION OF GLASS PATTERNS

Who made it? At one time or another this is a question to which all antique glassware collectors seek a specific answer. It is one of the most difficult questions to satisfy, and can contain some serious pitfalls particularly as related to pattern glass.

We are no smarter than the many writers that have preceded us, and readily admit that the identifications methods used involve no new innovations. For example, we have relied upon old catalogs and trade advertisements, trademarks, signatures, museums, design patent information, cautious analysis and knowledgeable authorities. In this latter case, there have been few individuals that we have known personally to be able to utilize their expertise.

The practice of attributing glass patterns to a particular glass house based upon glass shards unearthed at an old abandoned factory site should not form a basis for positive attribution. Several notable authorities have exposed why such methods are unreliable. If the reader wishes to communicate with us, we will be happy to supply chapter and verse as strong back-up to this opinion. Such attribution techniques are not used by us.

After utilization of all possible analytical approaches and processes of elimination, one is still faced with the fact that American glass houses copied each other's popular patterns, traded molds, were absorbed into larger corporations that reissued patterns at a later date, employed skilled designers and glass makers that had migrated, for one reason or another, from competitive glass companies. All of which makes attribution extremely difficult and in some cases essentially impossible.

With over twenty years of specialized glass collecting experience behind us, using many old pieces for comparison, every effort has been made to be as accurate as possible. Still, many of the salt shakers in our collection contain unanswerable criteria necessary for pattern attribution. Therefore, we did the next best thing and placed these patterns in our "POTPOURRI" section in alphabetical order by pattern name, with an approximate age of each piece (CIRCA). This latter step can be accomplished with reasonable accuracy when you have specialized for an extended period of time.

With full knowledge that perfection has not been achieved, we welcome any corrections, along with your substantiating data, so that corrective action can be taken.

SALT SHAKER TOPS

How does the serious collector know if the top on a shaker that he is about to purchase is an original? Most of the time he will not.

Should a collector purchase an old glass shaker if the top is missing? In our opinion, it is a mistake not to purchase a desired piece of ware simply because the top is missing. The few exceptions would be in the case of a shaker that has the identity obliterated due to lack of the original top. For example, "Owl, Little", "Mt. Washington Fig", "Mt. Washington Egg, Flat End" or "Tomato" are unique, and of such a specialized nature, that they would be of little, if any, value if their original tops are missing.

When a collector locates a desired shaker that has no top, it never hurts to bring it to the attention of the individual offering it for sale. Quite often this can form the basis for negotiation of the original asking price.

Through diligent search, we have many times secured a suitable old top for a glass shaker that was purchased at an earlier date. While one should remain cognizant of the type of exceptions previously mentioned, it is the glass itself, coupled with the scarcity factor, that generally determines the value of an old glass salt shaker.

PLATE I

ATTERBURY AND COMPANY PITTSBURGH, PA. 1859 - 1893

1. JOHNNY BULL [Mold Blown Opaque Glass]
CIRCA: 1873 - 1883
In 1873, Thomas B. Atterbury patented a saloon pepper designed to appear as a formally dressed gentleman, designated today as "Johnny Bull". According to an 1874 Atterbury Catalog, the saloon pepper was made in white-opaque glass only. RARE

BAKEWELL, PEARS AND COMPANY PITTSBURGH, PA. 1808 - 1882

2. OWL, LITTLE [Pressed Glass]
CIRCA: 1877 - 1882
The first design patent specifically for a salt shaker was patented in February, 1877, by H.P. Pears of Pittsburgh, Pa. The body was made of clear glass pressed and the head of pewter. Salt is dispensed through perforations in the back of the head. The Little Owl is among the rarest and most highly prized by collectors of pressed glassware. VERY RARE

BOSTON AND SANDWICH GLASS COMPANY SANDWICH, MASS.
1825 - 1888
3. BARREL, CHRISTMAS [Mold Blown Glass]
CIRCA: 1877 - 1888
This shaker measured 1 3/4 inches tall, and was patented by Dana K. Alden, of Boston, Mass., on Dec. 25, 1877. The patent date established the pattern name of this item. Some shakers contain an agitator, which was designed to have both longitudinal movement along with rotation to breakup encrusted salt. Many of the tops have been marked with the patent date, along with Alden's name. Colors observed are crystal, blue, vaseline, green, amethyst, amber, cranberry and milk-white opaque. This latter item is decorated with hand painted leaves. VERY SCARCE

4. LAFAYET SALT BOAT [Pressed Glass]
CIRCA: 1826 - 1828
This book is about salt shakers. However, we decided to include this piece due to its rarity, and to demonstrate that those so-called sleepers are still available. Widely recognized as a museum piece today, this open salt was acquired at a fraction of its monetary value in late 1974. The "Lafayet Boat Sandwich Salt" is known to have been manufactured in crystal, opaque white, opaque light blue, canary-yellow and sapphire-blue. There are two variants, one with beaded ornaments instead of "Sandwich" with scrolls on the base; the other contains a scroll ornament on the base and no "Sandwich" mark on the inside. During 1975, seven were displayed at the "Corning Museum of Glass, Corning N.Y.". This boat-shaped salt-celler is one of the very few, if not the only piece of glass signed at the Boston and Sandwich Glass Co. NO PRICE IS LISTED DUE TO EXTREMELY HIGH SCARCITY.

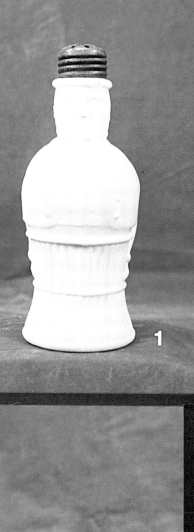

1

2

3

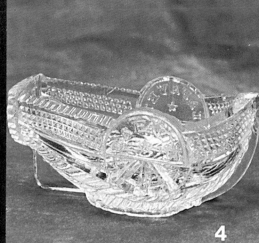

4

PLATE II

BRYCE BROTHERS MT. PLEASANT, PA. 1885 - 1892

1. ATLAS [Cannon Ball]   **[Mold Blown & Pressed Glass]**
CIRCA: 1885 - 1891
We are using the original pattern name, but this ware is also known as "Bullet" or "Cannon Ball". The shakers were produced in crystal and crystal with ruby. . . the latter will often be engraved with a name, place, and date since much of it was sold as souvenir glass. Some of these items will be found with an acid-etched floral design, as is the case with the shaker that we have illustrated.

BRYCE, HIGBEE AND COMPANY HOMESTEAD. PA. 1879 - 1907

2. BEEHIVE   **[Mold Blown & Pressed Opaque Glass]**
CIRCA: 1888 - 1898
A very unusual condiment dispenser with an octagon shaped base configured in the form of a beehive. There are six bees, in raised relief, positioned at various locations on the outside. We have no color experience to report in connection with this shaker. VERY SCARCE

BUCKEYE GLASS WORKS BRIDGEPORT, OHIO

3. OPAL-RIBBON, SHORT   **[Mold Blown Glass]**
CIRCA: 1888 - 1896
While really more of a type of swirl pattern, we are acknowledging and accepting the pattern name assigned by a previous author. Enough confusion already exists today because too many writers have decided to create a new name for a pattern, where one previously existed. This opalescent pattern was manufactured in a variety of pieces. Observed colors are blue, cranberry and white. Some shakers will be found with a satin finish. SCARCE

4. CHRYSANTHEMUM BASE   **[Mold Blown Glass]**
CIRCA: 1888 - 1892
This is another Harry Northwood product, 2 3/8 inches tall, containing a white ribbon opalescent swirl pattern. This same motif can be found in a speckled finish, and is considered to be the subject of a Northwood special patent. Observed in white, blue and cranberry. Occasionally found with a satin finish. The satin shakers are SCARCE.

PLATE III

CAMBRIDGE GLASS COMPANY CAMBRIDGE, OHIO 1901 - 1954

1. STAR OF BETHLEHEM [Pressed Glass]
CIRCA: 1909 - 1910

This pattern was known as the Cambridge Glass Company's No. 2656, and was illustrated in a trade catalog dated 1909. Glassware in this pattern was produced in approximately forty pieces.

CHALLINOR, TAYLOR AND COMPANY TARENTUM, PA. 1884 - 1891

2. CHALLINOR'S NO. 20. [Forget-Me-Not] [Mold Blown Opaque Glass]
CIRCA: 1885 - 1891

This is the original trade catalog listing for this pattern. Made in various opaque colors (we have never observed it in crystal) in a restricted number of items; condiment set, sugar shaker, cruet, syrup jug, and salt shakers. Challinor later became a part of the U.S. Glass Company.

CONSOLIDATED LAMP AND GLASS COMPANY PITTSBURGH AND CORAOPOLIS, PA. 1894 - 1967

3. BULGING THREE PETAL CONDIMENT [Mold Blown Cased Glass]
CIRCA: 1894 - 1900

We first discovered individual shakers in this pattern, and after approximately ten years acquired the complete condiment set, with its delicate glass holder, in pink cased glass. Unfortunately, we have noticed that these complete sets are now being reproduced, and the workmanship is excellent. Observed in pink, blue and yellow cased glass. VERY SCARCE IN A COMPLETE SET.

14

PLATE IV

CONSOLIDATED LAMP AND GLASS COMPANY PITTSBURGH AND CORAOPOLIS, PA. 1894 - 1967

1. BULGING LEAF   [Mold Blown Opaque Glass]
CIRCA: 1894 - 1896
An early catalog listed this pattern as No. 31. The motif consists of two rows of bulging leaves. Observed in blue, pink, white and green-opaque glass. Some shakers are cased. SCARCE

2. HALF CONE   [Mold Blown Cased Glass]
CIRCA: 1895 - 1900
This pattern appears to have had limited production. The motif divides the shaker into two sections; the upper portion is smooth, and lower two-thirds contain small overlapping cones in raised relief. Measuring 2 1/8 inches tall, this ware is considered RARE in yellow or pink cased glass.

3. COTTON BALE   [Mold Blown Opaque Glass]
CIRCA: 1894 - 1898
Quite an unusual configuration, the pattern name depicts an appropriate description of this shaker. Observed in white, blue, pink and green. It is possible that other colors were marketed. SCARCE

4. CONE   [Mold Blown Opaque Glass]
CIRCA: 1894 - 1905
The Cone pattern appears to have been quite popular. It was made in a variety of items for several years. It is available in all colors, cased and satin glass.

16

PLATE V

CONSOLIDATED LAMP AND GLASS COMPANY PITTSBURGH AND CORAOPOLIS, PA. 1894 - 1967

1. FLOWER ASSORTMENT   [Mold Blown Opaque Glass]
CIRCA: 1894 - 1897
An unusual pattern, each side of the shaker depicts a different type floral arrangement in raised relief. Observed in pink (some with a white shading) blue, white and green. SCARCE

2. GUTTATE   [Mold Blown Cased Glass]
CIRCA: 1894 - 1900
This is an intricate pattern. The shaker is now being reproduced with a two-piece metal top. The original types have glass threads designed for utilization of a single piece metal top. This major deviation from the original ware should not pose a problem to the advanced collector but new collectors could be taken in because the glass quality is quite good on the reproductions.

3. GUTTATE, SQUATTY   [Mold Blown Opaque Glass]
CIRCA: 1898 - 1900
With the discovery of an 1898 trade advertisement that illustrates this smaller variant of the basic Guttate pattern, it appears that a limited quantity of these shakers were distributed. Over the years we have observed very few; our color experience has been limited to white and pink. RARE

4. SHELL, OVERLAPPING   [Mold Blown Opaque Glass]
CIRCA: 1894 - 1900
This design reminds one of a type of sea shell, and the pattern name appears to be an excellent choice. Observed in white, pink (some cased), blue and green. Other colors probably exist. The cased shakers are SCARCE.

PLATE VI

DITHRIDGE AND CO., FORT PITT GLASS WORKS
PITTSBURGH, PA. 1857 - Closing date unknown

1. BULGE BOTTOM [Mold blown Opaque Glass]
CIRCA: 1894 - 1896
Usually found in white-opaque glass with painted poppies and leaves in raised relief. We have observed this ware in a solid blue-opaque homogenous glass. VERY SCARCE

2. CREASED BALE [Mold Blown Opaque Glass]
CIRCA: 1894 - 1905
In addition to individual shakers and a toothpick, this ware was manufactured in a three-piece condiment set containing a mustard with a matching glass tray. The tray is quite fragile, resulting in a low survival factor. Therefore, acquisition of a complete set is a bit of a challenge. We have observed a complete condiment set reproduced in custard glass, so it is possible that other colors are being reproduced. The craftsmanship is quite good. Collectors are advised to use caution. Observed colors are white, blue, custard, green and pink (all in opaque glass). Complete sets when located are VERY SCARCE.

3. HEART [Mold Blown Opaque Glass]
CIRCA: 1894 - 1897
We looked at this one carefully due to the unusual shadings of pink-to-white. It is certainly unique, but not a form of peachblow. Observed colors are white, blue, and pink (all in opaque glass). SCARCE

4. SCROLL AND SQUARE [Mold Blown Opaque Glass]
CIRCA: 1894 - 1898
Dithridge produced this pattern in a wide variety of opaque colors. The design apparently sold very well, as this pattern has been observed in green, white, pink, blue and custard.

1

2

3

4

PLATE VII

DITHRIDGE AND CO., FORT PITT GLASS WORKS PITTSBURGH, PA.
1857 - Closing Date Unknown

1. SPIDER WEB [Alba]   **[Mold Blown Opaque Glass]**
CIRCA: 1893 - 1898

An unusual and popular pattern. Observed colors are white, blue, pink and custard. The custard shakers are SCARCE.

2. SUNSET   **[Mold Blown Opaque Glass]**
CIRCA: 1894 - 1900

Listed as Dithridge No. 50 in a trade catalog, this pattern has been observed in white, blue, pink (some with a white shading) and custard. The custard shakers are VERY SCARCE.

3. SWIRL, DIAGONAL WIDE [NA]   **[Mold Blown Opaque Glass]**
CIRCA: 1894 - 1896

The motif consists of wide diagonal swirls which alternate from smooth to grooved. This item is listed as No. 56 in a trade catalog dated October 1894. Observed colors are white, blue and pink. SCARCE

4. TEARDROP BULGING   **[Mold Blown Opaque Glass]**
CIRCA: 1894 - 1900

Originally a part of a condiment set, this shaker has been observed in white, blue and custard. There are many reproductions. If one is not experienced in the identification of the Victorian Period Opaque, homogenous glass, care should be exercised. An original complete condiment set is considered VERY SCARCE.

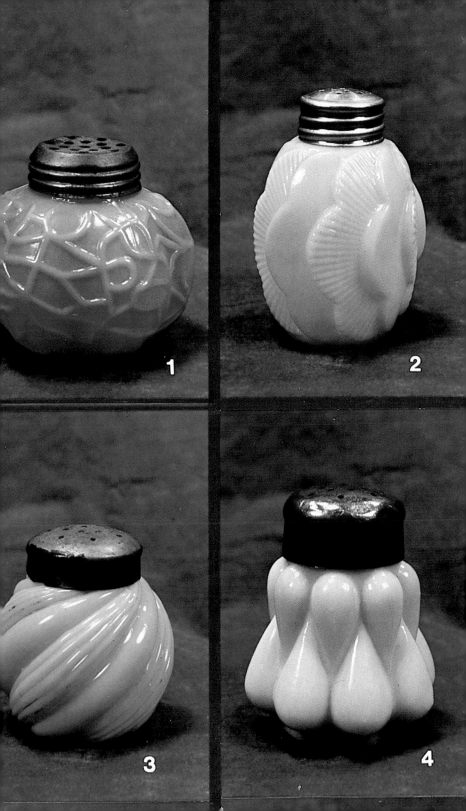

PLATE VIII

DITHRIDGE AND CO., FORT PITT GLASS WORKS, PITTSBURGH, PA.
1857 - Closing Date unknown

1. TORCH AND WREATH　　　　　　　　[Mold Blown Opaque Glass]
CIRCA: 1895 - 1904

This custard shaker has a distinctive lemon-yellow tint to it. If this pattern was produced in other table or novelty items, none have been observed or reported. Known colors are blue, pink-cased, white, green and custard. SCARCE

GEORGE A. DUNCAN AND SONS PITTSBURGH, PA. 1874 - 1886
DUNCAN AND HEISEY CO., PITTSBURGH, PA. 1886 - 1889

2. SHELL AND TASSEL [Square]　　　　　　　[Pressed Glass]
CIRCA: 1881 - 1889

This pattern was the design of A. H. Heisey during his association with George A. Duncan & Sons. He obtained his patent on July 26, 1881. For complete details, the reader is referred to pages 77, 78 and 79 of "Glass Patents and Patterns" by Arthur G. Peterson, who through diligent research, has at last straightened out the confusion of proper pattern attribution. The salt shakers are VERY SCARCE.

DUNCAN AND MILLER GLASS COMPANY, WASHINGTON, PA.
1901 - 1955 [Approx. closing Date]

3. BUTTON ARCHES　　　　　　　[Mold Blown & Pressed Glass]
CIRCA: 1901 - 1909

Prior to 1901, this firm was called "George Duncan's Sons and Co."; prior to 1894 this glass house was affiliated with the U. S. Glass Company. This pattern was very popular, and was distributed primarily in various pieces of "Souvenir" glass. The illustrated shaker is in Clambroth, and marked "Souvenir Junction City, Kansas". The pattern is being reproduced, but we have never seen a reproduced salt shaker. Observed in crystal, custard, clambroth, and ruby-flashed colors.

EAGLE GLASS AND MANUFACTURING CO.,
WELLSBURG, WEST VIRGINIA 1894 - 1925

4. BUTTERFLY　　　　　　　[Mold Blown and Pressed Glass]
CIRCA: 1898 - 1904

Measuring 2 5/8 inches tall, this opalware contains four butterflies in raised relief. Some can be found with the butterflies painted in various colors. SCARCE

SOUVENIR
nction City, Kas

PLATE IX

EAGLE GLASS AND MANUFACTURING CO., WELLSBURG, WEST VIRGINIA 1894 - 1925

1. COSMOS SCROLL CONDIMENT [NA] **[Mold Blown & Pressed Glass]**
CIRCA: 1899 - 1906

The matching tray that contains the salt, pepper and mustard is very fragile. Few appear to have survived. This set was made only in opaque opalware and decorated in various pastel colors which are carried over to each matching tray. We managed to collect the salts individually, but it was a number of years before a complete set was located. RARE as a complete set.

2. FLEUR-DE-LIS CONDIMENT [NA] **[Mold Blown & Pressed Glass]**
CIRCA: 1899 - 1903

The set consists of a tall salt and a short, somewhat squatty pepper, on an opalware tray. Early trade advertisements indicate that this ware was marketed only as a salt and pepper with small companion tray. A complete set is VERY SCARCE.

3. FLOWER BLOOMING **[Mold Blown & Pressed Glass]**
CIRCA: 1899 - 1905

Consisting of rather heavy opaque-white glass containing a gilt colored decoration, this shaker has been reproduced. Collectors should exercise caution.

4. FORGET-ME-NOT-PEEWEE AND COMPANION
[Mold Blown & Pressed Glass]
CIRCA: 1899 - 1905

Individual shakers are not too difficult to locate, but this ware was sold as a set with matching glass tray. Made in white and blue opaque glass, collecting a complete set is a bit of a challenge. SCARCE

1

2

3

4

PLATE X

FOSTORIA GLASS COMPANY MOUNDSVILLE, WEST VIRGINIA
1887 - Still in Business

1. TULIP BASE [Mold Blown Opaque Glass]
CIRCA: 1898 - 1904
Standing 2 5/8 inches tall, this shaker contains a large flower surrounded by green leaves repeated twice. The base contains six tulips, all in raised relief. VERY SCARCE

GILLINDER AND SONS PHILADELPHIA, PA.
1867 - [During 1890's Joined U.S. Glass Co.]

2. MELON [Mold Blown Satin Glass]
CIRCA: 1888 - 1892
We have used a sugar shaker to illustate this pattern. It is available to collectors in the salt and pepper. The motif consists of hand decorated satin glass configured in the form of a melon. The glass is thin & delicate, and contains the original silver (sterling) top.

T.G. HAWKES & COMPANY CORNING, NEW YORK
1868 - [Not certain of Closing Date]

3. DIAMOND & STAR [NA] [Heavy Cut Brilliant Crystal]
CIRCA: 1900 - 1910
An excellent example of the quality cut glass produced by this glass house. Standing 3 inches tall, the bottom contains the etched Hawkes trademark which consists of two hawkes in the lower two-thirds of a trefoiled ring. SCARCE

4. DIAMOND & ZIPPER [NA] [Heavy Cut Brilliant Crystal]
CIRCA: 1891 - 1900
The principal motif contains two diamonds separated by a vertical zipper. The neck contains six plain panels outlined with vertical beading. The shaker measures 2½ inches tall. SCARCE

1

2

3

4

PLATE XI

A.H. HEISEY AND COMPANY NEWARK, OHIO 1893 - 1956

1. IVORINA VERDE [Winged Scroll]   **[Mold Blown & Pressed Glass]**
CIRCA: 1901 - 1904

Often called "Winged Scroll", the original factory name was "Ivorina Verde". It is our opinion that original firm of manufacture names should be used if known. Observed colors are custard, opaque-white, green, vaseline and crystal. Full table settings were manufactured. The custard has been generally the most popular with collectors. We have never seen a piece with the "Diamond H" trademark because it was not patented until 1906, and the majority of this ware was manufactured prior to that time. The custard salt shakers should be considered RARE.

2. PUNTY BAND [Heisey #1220]   **[Mold Blown & Pressed Glass]**
CIRCA: 1896 - 1908

This is an excellent example of the off-white opaque-glass imitative of the color of milk and egg custard, commonly known as "Custard Glass". The "Diamond H" will often be found on the inside-bottom of the salt shakers. Observed colors are crystal, ruby-flashed and custard (as illustrated). VERY SCARCE

PLATE XII

HOBBS, BROCKUNIER AND COMPANY, WHEELING, WEST VIRGINIA
1845 - 1891

1. ACORN   [Mold Blown Opaque Glass]
CIRCA: 1889 - 1891
This design was originated by Knicholas Kopp Jr. during his association with this glass house. Observed in white, blue, pink-with-white-shading and black.
A slight variant shaker, having a more narrow bredith, and made in both opaque and non-opaque glass can also be collected. This latter ware is a product of a different manufacturer that we have been unable to identify. The Hobbs black-opaque shakers appear to have had a limited production, and are RARE. The shaded white-to-pink are SCARCE.

2. PILLAR, SIXTEEN   [Lattice Ribbed][Mold Blown Glass]
CIRCA: 1885 - 1890
An opalescent pattern containing sixteen vertical pillars, and a white lattice diamond network. We have overheard some individuals mistakenly call this ware "Spatter Glass". Observed in white, cranberry and blue (all opalescent) colors. VERY SCARCE

3. SWIRL, OPALESCENT   [Mold Blown Glass]
CIRCA: 1890 - 1894
Here is a quality shaker. The principal motif consists of cranberry coloring with opalescent ribbon swirls. Observed in blue, cranberry and crystal; all containing white ribbon swirls. SCARCE

4. THUMBPRINT INVERTED, ROUND   [Mold Blown and Pressed Glass]
CIRCA: 1880 - 1888
Hobbs was a major producer of this pattern. It has been the subject of many reproductions. The beginning collector should exercise caution. An excellent quality reproduction is being imported from Europe; even the experts are having their problems with it. This is particularly true in cranberry and amberina. The salt shakers are SCARCE.

PLATE XIII
IMPERIAL GLASS COMPANY, BELLAIRE, OHIO
1901 - Present

1. GRAPE CARNIVAL   **[Mold Blown and Pressed Glass]**
CIRCA: 1965 - 1970
While this is a late shaker in Rubigold Carnival, we do consider it collectible. It is also made in Peacock Carnival glass. Imperial has impressed its current trademark of IG upon the bottom (the letter I bisects the G). Imperial has produced this ware on a limited basis.

2. JOHNNY BULL   **[Mold Blown and Pressed Glass]**
CIRCA: 1960 - 1963
A reproduction of the Atterbury Saloon Pepper of 1873, which was originally made only in milk-white opaque glass. This shaker was made in both Rubigold and Peacock carnival; the Imperial IG trademark has been applied to the bottom. Arthur G. Peterson has reported that a few were reproduced in the milk-white glass during the 1950 era, but we have never observed any of them. Since the majority have been made in carnival glass, they pose no threat to the original Atterbury shaker.

3. MARY BULL   **[Mold Blown and Pressed Glass]**
CIRCA: 1960 - 1963
This special design by Imperial is considered to be a companion to the carnival Johnny Bull shaker. It was produced in both Rubigold and Peacock carnival glass with the IG trademark.

4. SPHINX   **[Mold Blown and Pressed Glass]**
CIRCA: 1910 - 1920
This unusual figural condiment shaker stands 3 ¼ inches tall. We have only observed one other, and it was in a private collection. The glass is of a rather heavy design, and survival from breakage should be very good. Despite this, it has remained obscure and most difficult to collect. Made in crystal only. RARE

1

2

3

4

PLATE XIV

INTERNATIONAL SILVER COMPANY, MERIDEN, CONNECTICUT
1898 - Present

HYBRID   **[Mold Blown & Pressed Glass]**
CIRCA: 1893 - 1905

While we have not been able to definitely establish which of the many silver firms in Meriden first marketed this ware, we have established that International Silver distributed these shakers after 1898. Patented on October 31, 1893 by E. A. Parker, Meriden, Connecticut, design patent 507,720. Many will be found with the patent date stamped near the bottom of the various covers; some are just stamped EPNS. This ware consists of a glass tube, containing an intaglio twelve-point rayed-star upon the bottom. An outside metal cylinder slides over the glass tube, and screws onto the threaded glass base. The metal cylinders consist of three types: solid metal (the most common); open scrolled near the top and bottom; bulbous shaped, with nine openings in the shape of a spear-head top and bottom. This latter type is quite SCARCE, and previously unlisted. We have illustrated all three types along with a view of a metal cylinder balanced upon top of a glass tube.

1

2

3

4

PLATE XV

THE JEFFERSON GLASS COMPANY STEUBENVILLE, OHIO
1900 - 1907

1. CIRCLE, DOUBLE
CIRCA: 1902 - 1906
Originally recorded as Jefferson's No. 231, this is a challenging pattern to collect. Observed only in green and blue containing an opalescent sheen. RARE

2. IRIS [Iris With Meander]   [Mold Blown and Pressed Glass]
CIRCA: 1904 - 1906
The original catalog name of this pattern was "Iris". In our opinion, the alternate name "Iris With Meander" more properly describes this item. An early catalog indicates that this pattern was made in blue, green, wine and crystal-with-gold decoration. However, we have never observed any wine colored shakers. VERY SCARCE. If the wine color exists, such shakers should be considered RARE.

3. RIBBED THUMBPRINT   [Pressed Glass]
CIRCA: 1905 - 1907
This popular pattern was sold primarily as souvenirs. It will be found frequently in the ruby-flashed glass as illustrated. Our shaker is dated 1905. . .an indication that this pattern was made at the Steubenville plant of Jefferson Glass Company prior to their move to Follansbee, W. Va. during 1907. The shaker stands 2 7/8 inches tall. Some will be found with the trademark Krys-Tol on the bottom. Observed in crystal, ruby-flashed, custard and blue. The custard shakers are VERY SCARCE.

4. SWAG WITH BRACKETS
CIRCA: 1902 - 1905
This has been a difficult pattern to collect. While other authors have reported numerous colors available, our observations indicate limited color production in salt shakers. Observed in crystal, blue and amethyst. We have been unable to verify any in opalescent colors. RARE

PLATE XVI

LALIQUE GLASS COMPANY, PARIS, FRANCE 1906 - Present

1. LALIQUE INTAGLIC [NA]   **[French Art Glass]**
CIRCA: 1915 - 1925

This is a frosted, cut, art glass of the twentieth Century made by Rene Lalique, of Paris, France. He originally concerned himself with the making of unique and unusual perfume flacons. A widely recognized maker of art glass who combined frosting, cutting, molding, pressing and free blowing to achieve his original designs. Many pieces contain his trademark, which is applied by acid etching. SCARCE

W.L. LIBBEY AND SONS COMPANY, TOLEDO, OHIO
1888 - 1892 - [Became Libbey Glass Co.]

2. DICE   **[Mold Blown Opaque Glass]**
CIRCA: 1889 - 1891

This unique shaker was patented by Joseph Locke in December 1889 as "A Condiment Holder". Joseph Lock migrated to the U. S. from England in 1882, securing a position with the New England Glass Company which closed down after a strike in 1888. Locke is credited with the invention, and subsequent patents of a variety of art glass, among which were Amberina, Agata, Pomona and Maize. This latter glass was patented in the Fall of 1889, and assigned to W.L. Libbey and Sons Co., of Toledo, Ohio; the firm with which Locke was then associated. We have injected this bit of history to illustrate the versatility of Locke and his ability to create unusual designs. The DICE shaker is no exception, and is considered to be RARE.

1

2

PLATE XVII

McKEE GLASS COMPANY, JEANNETTE, PA.
1903 - 1951

1. INTAGLIO SWIRL
CIRCA: 1908 - 1915
A 3 inch tall shaker, containing two gilt-colored sunken flowers between two leafy vines in raised-relief. We have no additional color experience to report.

2. FLOWER PANEL   [Mold Blown Opaque Glass]
CIRCA: 1904 - 1912
This item is an excellent example of the confusion that is created when deciding upon pattern attribution. Dithridge made an almost identical pattern. No attempt will be made to indicate who possibly copied who. Our attribution is based upon a very clear illustration found in an old McKee catalog. The motif consists of an unusual hexagon-shaped design; every other beaded panel contains a leaf-type design. All that we have observed are of white-opaque painted as described. SCARCE

3. SCROLLED NECK WITH PLUME[NA]   [Mold Blown Opaque Glass]
CIRCA: 1903 - 1910
We believe that the assigned pattern name adequately describes this item. With a height of 3 3/8 inches, this shaker was produced and decorated in various colors. It is unfortunate that our illustrated example no longer contains the original painted colors. Time, and no doubt many washings have obliterated the paints. VERY SCARCE

4. COLONIAL, ENGLISH   [Pressed Glass]
CIRCA: 1900 - 1912
Originally listed as pattern #75, the earlier pieces will be found with the trademark "PRESCUT". A high quality, brilliant, crystal shaker; it measures 3¼ inches tall. This pattern was produced in a variety of table pieces for at least two decades, perhaps longer.

1

2

3

4

PLATE XVIII

MEISSEN FACTORIES, MEISSEN, GERMANY
1709 - Present

1. MEISSEN [Quality German Porcelain]
CIRCA: 1895 - 1910

Often referred to as the ware that most closely approximates Chinese porcelain, and claimed as a German invention, but actually a chance discovery by E. W. Tachirnhausen and J. F. Bottger, the latter an alchemist and fakir who under the pretext of requiring better crucibles for his secret of making lead into gold, found the crucibles that he made were porcelain. This shaker is quite representative of the fine, translucent, hard earthenware china that is marketed and exported from the German Meissen Factories. Standing 3 3/8 inches tall, this item was part of a complete condiment set. VERY SCARCE

C.F. MONROE COMPANY, MERIDEN, CONN. 1894 - 1918

2. SCROLL, WAVE
CIRCA: 1895 - 1900

The "Wavecrest" trademark was patented on May 31, 1898. These products were decorated and distributed by C. F. Monroe Company from around 1895 to 1918. Since this Company was not a glass manufacturer, they purchased blown and pressed blank opalware from abroad, and from the Pairpoint Corporation of New Bedford, Mass. The salt shakers should be considered SCARCE.

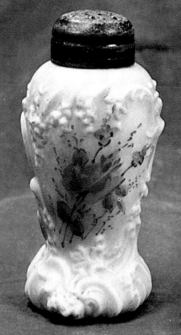

PLATE XIX

MT. WASHINGTON GLASS COMPANY,
NEW BEDFORD, MASSACHUSETTS 1869 - 1894

1. CROWN MILANO   [Mold Blown Art Glass]

CIRCA: 1893 - 1896

"Crown Milano" was patented in 1893. It is found in both marked and unmarked pieces. When marked, the trademark consists of the letters CM with a crown above them. The illustrated shaker consists of satinized opaque glass. VERY SCARCE

2. EGG, FLAT END   [Mold Blown Art Glass]

CIRCA: 1889 - 1897

This shaker was design patented during May 1889 by Albert Steffin. It is usually found in opaque glass and individually hand decorated. We have never seen a pair containing identical matching decorations. Known to have been made in white-opaque, custard and cut crystal. A Burmese shaker has been reported, but not verified by the authors.

3. EGG, FLAT SIDE   [Mold Blown Art Glass]

CIRCA: 1893 - 1896

This ware was patented during April 1893, by Alfred E. Smith. While manufactured by Mt. Mashington, shakers can be found with a "Libbey Glass" paper label because a large quantity was made for them for selling at the "1893 Columbian Exhibition". This type of shaker was made by blowing a gather of milk-white glass into full size molds, with a subsequent acidized treatment to attain a satin finish, after which, hand enameled decorations were applied. SCARCE

4. PILLAR RIBBED   [Mold Blown Satin Glass]

CIRCA: 1885 - 1895

This basic shaped pattern was made by Mt. Washington for several years. Perhaps the earliest manufacture was in "Burmese", which is the most expensive to obtain. The illustrated satin shaker has the decorative colors fired onto it. SCARCE

1

2

3

4

PLATE XX

MT. WASHINGTON GLASS COMPANY,
NEW BEDFORD, MASSACHUSETTS 1869 - 1894

1. FLORAL SPRAY [NA]   [Mold Blown Opaque Satin Glass]
CIRCA: 1884 - 1890
This shaker, as far as we have been able to determine, has not been previously listed in any other publication. It contains a hand decorated floral spray as its principal motif. This ware has also been observed in "Burmese". VERY SCARCE

2. LOBE FIVE   [Mold Blown Opaque Satin Glass]
CIRCA: 1885 - 1892
This hand decorated item contains various floral designs. As in the manner of the "Tomato" and "Fig", an identically decorated pair would be RARE.

3. SCROLL AND BULGE   [Mold Blown Opaque Satin Glass]
CIRCA: 1888 - 1894
Triangular in shape, with three oblong bulging panels, each of which is decorated with a hand-painted floral spray. SCARCE

4. TWO FLOWER SPRIG [NA]   [Mold Blown Opaque Glass]
CIRCA: 1885 - 1890
Consisting of a two-piece pewter top, and a motif of two hand-painted flowers on a single branch containing brown leaves; the glass is homogenous with a mother-of-pearl finish. This item is 2¼ inches tall to the top of the metal collar with top removed. We have never observed another shaker of this design. VERY RARE

1

2

3

4

PLATE XXI

MT. WASHINGTON GLASS COMPANY,
NEW BEDFORD, MASSACHUSETTS 1869 - 1894

1. FLORAL DOME [NA]   [Mold Blown Satin Glass]
CIRCA: 1892 - 1894

The typical hand painted floral decorations, along with the spring-like tapered top, establish this ware as a Mt. Washington product. The principal motif is a triangular shaped dome with a flat bottom that contains an intaglio circle 3/4 inches in diameter. VERY SCARCE

2. FIG   [Mold Blown Art Glass]
CIRCA: 1893 - 1894

A truly ornate art glass shaker, this ware is sometimes referred to by collectors as an "Onion Shaker". It was patented in 1893 by Albert Steffin during his association with Mt. Washington. The unusual spring-like tapering top, along with variations, are reflected on other Mt. Washington shakers (see figs. 1 and 3). The FIG can be found in various colors and shades, each will be individually hand decorated. Probably due to cost, they appear to have been marketed (priced) individually, for we have never seen two that were identically decorated. A perfectly matched pair would be RARE.

3. EGG, FLAT END VARIANT [NA]   [Mold Blown Art Glass]
CIRCA: 1892 - 1894

This shaker represents a variation of the spring-like tapering top that was patented by Mt. Washington for the "FIG" shaker. The motif consists of hand-painted enamel floral decorations applied over custard glass. We really got excited when we found this one, because first appearances suggested that the glass was "Glossy Burmese", since Mt. Washington is not generally considered a producer of custard glass. A recent telephone call from a collector friend informed us that another author has named this item "Ostrich Egg", since a sugar shaker is being illustrated. However, careful comparison indicates that the name established by Arthur G. Peterson is more applicable to the salt shaker. RARE

4. ROYAL FLEMISH [NA]   [Mold Blown Art Glass]
CIRCA: 1893 - 1894

A rare art glass that was patented by Albert Steffin on February 27, 1894. It is interesting to note the similarity to the vertically fluted (veined) glass of the Mt. Washington "FIG". Credit must be given to Victor W. Buck, of Upland, California for identification of this piece. We believe, but are not 100% certain, that this ware was called "Bark, Translucent" by Arthur G. Peterson. VERY RARE

PLATE XXII

MT. WASHINGTON GLASS COMPANY
NEW BEDFORD, MASSACHUSETTS 1869 - 1894

1. LEAF, BERRY FOUR FEET [NA]   **[Mold Blown Art Glass]**
CIRCA: 1887 - 1894

This shaker consists of a delicate satinized opalware. The motif reflects hand-decorated green leaves on a vine sprouting orange berries that are somewhat reminicent of holly. An ornate flower and scrolled pattern in raised-relief, encircles the top and base of the shakers which has four small feet. RARE

2. LOOP AND DAISY   **[Mold Blown Art Glass]**
CIRCA: 1886 - 1893

A fragile shaker, 2 5/8 inches tall, and made of excellent quality satin glass. The principal motif consists of two large hand-painted daisy and vine sprigs spread across six looping panels. The base is formed by six scallop-shaped feet. A delicate salmon-colored background complements the total design. VERY SCARCE

3. EGG IN CUP   **[Mold Blown Art Glass]**
CIRCA: 1885 - 1890

Standing 2 1/8 inches tall, this shaker contains the typical Mt. Washington hand-applied floral decorating styles. The metal top is of a special design and unique. The shaker has little value without it. RARE

4. LOBE, SQUATTY   **[Mold Blown Art Glass]**
CIRCA: 1888 - 1893

This is a design variation of the "Tomato", and should be credited to Albert Steffin. The two-piece metal top contains a leafy design, and is identical in configuration to that of the "Tomato" salt shaker. Individually hand-decorated, an identically decorated pair would be rare. SCARCE

PLATE XXIII

MT. WASHINGTON GLASS COMPANY,
NEW BEDFORD, MASSACHUSETTS 1869 - 1894

1. TOMATO [Mold Blown Art Glass]
CIRCA: 1889 - 1894
This shaker was patented in 1889 by Albert Steffin as a tomato design. Some collectors refer to it as a squatty melon. Found in colors of white, pink and tan, with various pastel shadings, they are always hand decorated (some by the Smith Brothers). The illustrated tan-shaded shaker is of special interest, because it is "Undeveloped Burmese", which has considerable more value than the more common tomato salts. Few collectors or dealers recognize this glass, since the normal finished Burmese is a soft canary-yellow, shading to flesh pink. Mt. Washington produced limited quantities of "Undeveloped Burmese". The white satin glass tomato is the more common; blue are VERY SCARCE; Undeveloped Burmese are RARE.

2. TOMATO, LARGE [NA] [Mold Blown Art Glass]
CIRCA: 1889 - 1891
Considerably larger in size, but of the same physcial configuration as the Tomato Salt Shaker, this muffineer was decorated by the Smith Brothers. In a blue, satinized glass, as illustrated, this sugar shaker is VERY SCARCE.

3. BIRD ARBOR [Mold Blown Art Glass]
CIRCA: 1886 - 1890
This shaker measures 4 inches tall to the top-edge of the metal collar that forms a part of the two-piece pewter top. This item consists of a light-yellow opaque inner-glass, that is covered by a clear outside layer of vaseline glass. Such ware is commonly referred to as cased-glass. The principal motif, all in hand applied enamelling, depicts a large bird on a branch backed by two painted circles. RARE

4. LOBE, SIX [NA] [Mold Blown Art Glass]
CIRCA: 1888 - 1894
Each of the six bulging panels contain a hand painted floral spray; three panels have a single flower and the others contain two. The shaker is 2 5/8 inches tall. SCARCE

1

2

3

4

PLATE XXIV

NATIONAL GLASS COMPANY, PITTSBURGH, PA.
1899 - [See text below]

1. ORINDA [Pressed Glass]
CIRCA: 1901 - 1910
We have purposely not listed a closing date for this Corporation because it consisted of at least twelve glass houses (factories). This pattern was produced at the Lancaster, Ohio plant. Observed colors are white opaque and crystal. We have had reports of production in ruby-flashed, none have been seen in salt shakers. SCARCE

2. S REPEAT [Mold Blown & Pressed Glass]
CIRCA: 1901 - 1910
A very popular pattern, but the market is heavily flooded with reproductions today. This ware was originally produced in crystal, blue, green and ametheyst. While we are aware that certain table pieces were produced in opalescent colors, no opalescent salt shakers have been observed. SCARCE

NEW MARTINSVILLE GLASS MFG. COMPANY, NEW MARTINSVILLE, OHIO 1901 - 1944

3. CURVED BODY [Mold Blown Opaque Glass]
CIRCA: 1905 - 1913
An unusual hand decorated white opaque opalware; each respective shaker has a painted floral design arranged in such a manner that either an "S" or "P" is formed upon it. Many glass houses coined fancy trade-names for their products. New Martinsville was no exception, since this ware was lumped under the title of "Muranese Glass"; a broad terminology used with several types of their glass during their early years. SCARCE

4. MANY PETALS [Mold Blown Opaque Glass]
CIRCA: 1902 - 1910
Containing a soft satin-like finish with many small flowers in raised relief, this shaker was categorized as "Muranese Glass". No doubt produced in other colors. VERY SCARCE

1

2

3

4

PLATE XXV

NEW ENGLAND GLASS COMPANY, CAMBRIDGE, MASS.
1818 - 1888

1. BLOSSOMTIME VARIANT [NA]   [Mold Blown Art Glass]
CIRCA: 1875 - 1885
Hand decorated, this shaker consists of a dual pattern; smooth barrel-shaped on the outside with vertical ribbing on the inside. Detailed examination of our shaker has disclosed that one or two of the floral petals have lost some enamel paint leaving an intaglio impression visible on the glass in an exact likeness of the painted floral design. This is an indication, perhaps, that the flower impressions were originally designed into the glass mold as an aid to subsequent hand decoration. The salt shaker contained a metal "Richardson Agitator" which was designed to break-up any lumpy salt formations. VERY RARE

2. MOTHER-OF-PEARL RAINDROP   [Mold Blown Art Glass]
CIRCA: 1880 - 1885
Sometimes referred to as "Pearl Satin-Ware", this pattern was formed by a so-called "Air-Trap" method, which required considerable skill and crafts-manship. Triple cased, with hand enamel decorations, the shaker shades from white at the bottom, to a rose color at the top. This item is fitted with a two-piece pewter top. RARE

3. NEW ENGLAND PEACHBLOW   [Mold Blown Art Glass]
CIRCA: 1886 - 1888
A homogenous glass shading from white and ivory tints to a deep rose. This ware was originally patented March 2, 1886 by Edward D. Libbey and marketed under the tradename "Wild Rose". We are of the opinion that the salt shakers were created only to special order and not produced in commercial quantities. VERY RARE

4. RUBINA [NA]   [Mold Blown Art Glass]
CIRCA: 1880 - 1888
This shaker stands 2 3/4 inches tall, and has a two-piece pewter top; hand decorated with a slender branch containing dainty buds interspersed among 12 leaves. It has an acidized finish that shades from a camphor (frosted) color at the bottom, to a deep rose at the top. RARE

PLATE XXVI

Because of the various opinions surrounding the glass patterns attributed to Harry Northwood, it appears to be a good idea to list the known glass houses with which he was associated during his brilliant career.

La Bell Glass Works, Bridgeport, Ohio 1886
Buckeye Glass Works, Bridgeport, Ohio .... 1887 - 1896
Northwood Glass Works, Martins Ferry, Ohio .... 1888 - 1895
The Northwood Company, Ellwood, Pa 1895
The Northwood Company, Indiana, Pa 1897
Northwood Glass Works, Indiana, Pa 1898
National Glass Companies (merger), Indiana, Pa 1900
The Harry Northwood Company, Wheeling, W. Va .... 1902 - 1913

* * * * * * *

NORTHWOOD GLASS WORKS, MARTINS FERRY, OHIO
1888 - 1895

1. CHRYSANTHEMUM SPRIG　　　　　　　**[Mold Blown & Pressed Glass]**
CIRCA: 1888 - 1895

The consensus of opinion indicates that this item was first produced in the late eighteen-eighties by Northwood. The reader is referred to the above Northwood career date, and invited to prove otherwise. It would be a massive under-taking. The salt shakers are three inches high and 2¼ inches in diameter. The custard shaker is VERY SCARCE: the blue-opaque are RARE.

THE NORTHWOOD COMPANY, INDIANA, PA.
1897 - 1898

2. ALASKA　　　　　　　　　　　　　　　**[Mold Blown Glass]**
CIRCA: 1897

This ware was made in a large variety of tableware, as well as salt and pepper shakers. While other colors have been reported, we have only observed the shakers, in blue and vaseline-opalescent. SCARCE

3. ALASKA VARIANT [NA]　　　　　　　　**[Mold Blown Glass]**
CIRCA: 1897

The pattern is the same as fig. 2, except that the outside is decorated with painted gold flowers. As previously indicated, our color experience indicates only the blue and vaseline-opalescent shakers. VERY SCARCE

THE HARRY NORTHWOOD COMPANY, WHEELING, WEST VIRGINIA
1902 - 1913

4. CIRCLED SCROLL　　　　　　　　　　**[Mold Blown & Pressed Glass]**
CIRCA: 1902 - 1905

The bulbous shaker measures 3 inches tall, and the bottoms contain a rough pontil mark. Our color experience amounts to only the blue and green salt shakers. RARE

PLATE XXVII

THE HARRY NORTHWOOD COMPANY, WHEELING, WEST VIRGINIA
1902 - 1913

1. JEWEL AND FLOWER   [Mold Blown & Pressed Glass]
CIRCA: 1903 - 1908

This opalescent glass pattern was made in a variety of tableware. However, the salt shakers are a challenge to collect. With a measured height of 3 inches, our color experience has been limited to the blue and vaseline opalescent shakers. RARE

2. EVERGLADES   [Mold Blown Glass]
CIRCA: 1903 - 1906

The appearance of this ware is most unusual. The composition consists of both purple-slag and clambroth-like glass. Standing 3¼ inches tall, this pattern was named by Robert Batty, of Little Rock, Arkansas. Various opalescent colors are known to exist in other types of tableware, but the shakers seem to be limited to the illustrated coloring and a light blue opalescent. VERY SCARCE

RICHARDS AND HARTLEY TARENTUM, PA.
1878 - 1892 Became Part of U. S. Glass

3. RICHMOND   [Pressed Glass]
CIRCA: 1880 - 1889

Produced only in crystal, this is the original pattern name assigned by the manufacturer. A wide range of tableware was distributed in this pattern. SCARCE

PAIRPOINT GLASS COMPANY, NEW BEDFORD, MASS. 1894 - 1938

GUNDERSON GLASS WORKS NEW BEDFORD, MASS. 1939 - 1952

4. CORNUCOPIA   [Quality Blown Crystal]
CIRCA: 1939 - 1949

This ware was produced in crystal only, and probably sold with a silver-plated stand designed to hold a pair of these shakers. The motif consists of sharp ribbing that divides each of the vertical panels. This, and similar ware of the Gunderson Glass Works, were produced in an attempt to compete with such fine glass houses as the Steuben Glass Co., of Corning, N. Y., which firm turned to the production of high quality crystal in 1933. An identical "Cornucopia" perfume was also made which had two glass feet that allowed it to stand upright. SCARCE

PLATE XXVIII

THE RIVERSIDE GLASS WORKS, WELLSBURG, WEST VIRGINIA
1879 - 1899

1. CROESUS   **[Mold Blown & Pressed Glass]**
CIRCA: 1897 - 1899

Due to the fact that this has become such a popular pattern, prices have advanced sharply, and the market is now being fed with excellent reproductions. Caution should be exercised prior to purchase. The attribution period to Riverside Glass is short, due to the merger with many other glass houses that comprised the National Glass Co., in late 1899. This pattern was produced in green, crystal and amethyst and most, but not all pieces contain gold decoration. The salt shakers are SCARCE in green, RARE in amethyst.

2. EMPRESS   **[Mold Blown & Pressed Glass]**
CIRCA: 1898 - 1899

In terms of artistic appeal, we believe that this pattern is of greater interest than Croesus. It is certainly more collectible, as it has not been reproduced. We have only observed this pattern in crystal and emerald green. However, as there have been reports of pieces in amethyst, there must have been some limited production.

3. X-RAY   **[Mold Blown & Pressed Glass]**
CIRCA: 1896 - 1899

This ware consists of rather thick, heavy, emerald green glass with gold decorations. While this is the original factory name, the pattern design in no way relates to it. We have observed this shaker in crystal and emerald green. There have been reports that the shakers were also made in amethyst, and if so, the latter should be considered RARE. VERY SCARCE

ROGERS, SMITH AND COMPANY MERIDEN, CONN. 1857 - 1918

4. LONGWY   **[French Pottery, Hand Decorated Staniferrous Paint]**
CIRCA: 1870 - 1885

Pronounced as "lung-vee", this ware was imported from a French Pottery in Longwy, France, and distributed in the U.S.A. by Rogers, Smith & Co. Found in various patterns, usually with small hand painted flowers forming a principal part of the motif. Some pieces will be found signed with the word "longwy" impressed upon the bottom. The shakers should be considered VERY SCARCE.

PLATE XXIX

SEVRES FACTORY, SEVRES, FRANCE 1753 - Present

1. SEVRES [NA]   [Quality French Porcelain]
CIRCA: 1915 - 1925

The town of Sevres, France, is famous for the production of fine porcelain. This shaker certainly upholds that tradition in every respect. The original factory was at Vincennes, but was established at Sevres in 1753 as The Royal Manufactory. The motif consists of lavender and gold at the top & bottom, with a white center containing hand painted enamel floral designs. The base and metal top are of Sterling Silver. VERY SCARCE

SMITH BROTHERS, NEW BEDFORD, MASS.
1871 - 1885 Decorators for Mt. Washington Glass Co.
1885 - closing date uncertain. Continued Decorating for Pairpoint

2. CABIN IN THE SNOW
CIRCA: 1888 - 1892

Alfred E. and Harry Smith established the glass decorating department at the Mt. Washington Glass Co., during 1871. They opened their own firm in New Bedford in 1885. The Brothers became well known for outstanding excellence in the application of enamelling on both satin & opalware glass. The illustrated salt shaker is very typical of their decorating expertise. The Brothers continued to do decorative work for Pairpoint Corp. up into the turn of the 20th Century. VERY SCARCE

3. LEAF AND SPEAR [NA]   [Mold Blown Art Glass]
CIRCA: 1894 - 1898

Smith Brothers decoration on a blank that was probably furnished by Mt. Washington Glass Co., the motif depicts leafy type decorations in relief, with eight small vertical spears pointing upward near the top. This shaker is shown on page 92 of a "Marshall Field Co." catalog as part of a lunch caster set priced at $3.30. SCARCE

STEUBEN GLASS COMPANY, CORNING, NEW YORK 1918 - Present

4. STEUBEN CRYSTAL [NA]
CIRCA: 1934 - 1938

In 1933, A. A. Houghton Jr. took over the Steuben Division. Under his management a high quality cyrstal clear glass has been, and is still being produced.
produced. The bottom of this ware is signed by a craftsman utilizing a diamond point, and writing the word "Steuben". It is a signature and not a trademark. This shaker measures 2¼ inches tall, and has a two-piece sterling silver top. Each shaker was completely hand-crafted, so the asking price was high at the time of manufacture. VERY SCARCE

1

2

3

4

PLATE XXX

UNITED STATES GLASS COMPANY VARIOUS LOCATIONS
1891 - Present [Factories A through T]

1. IOWA   [Mold Blown & Pressed Glass]
CIRCA: 1900 - 1903

A pattern consisting of bulging panels with zipper type separations. The panels are crystal with each zipper containing gilt decoration. Occasionally, this ware may be found in a pink-flashed color. The shakers were made in two sizes. The basic pattern was manufactured in a complete set of tableware. SCARCE

2. MANHATTAN   [Mold Blown & Pressed Glass]
CIRCA: 1902 - 1904

We are not certain which of the approximately twenty factories made this pattern, but a full set of tableware can be collected with patience. Known colors are crystal and red-flashed. VERY SCARCE

WEST VIRGINIA GLASS COMPANY, MARTINS FERRY, OHIO,
1890 - 1898
3. POLKA DOT   [Mold Blown Opalescent Glass]
CIRCA: 1891 - 1897

There are differences of opinion as to the original designer of this pattern. Variations can be found, and reproductions exist. In our opinion, the shaker we illustrated is properly attributed. Visual inspection is reminiscent of a cameo-type ware, however, the motif consists of an inner-layer of blue glass that is covered by an outer-layer of opalescent glass. The special molding technique employed reveals the blue glass in the form of circular dots, sometimes called thumbprints. RARE

THOMAS WEBB AND SONS, STOURBRIDGE, ENGLAND

4. WEBB PEACHBLOW [NA]   [Mold Blown Art Glass]
CIRCA: 1880 - 1885

Fitted with a two-piece pewter top, very few of these shakers were made, and probably only to special orders. The manufacturers, Thomas Webb and Sons, operated their glass house at Stourbridge, England. The quality of their glass ranks among the finest made. VERY RARE

PLATE XXXI

POTPOURRI

This section has been created for listing and illustrating, in alphabetical order by pattern name, those shakers that we have been unable to attribute to a particular glass house. After careful research, those patterns that have not been named in previous antique publications, have been assigned names. This action is designated by use of the acronym (NA) following each title, indicating "Named By Authors". Where height dimensions are listed, they were measured with the top removed from each shaker. We have tried to indicate the various colors of each shaker we have listed based primarily upon our own personal obsersvations.

1. APRICOT BAND[Eight Ball Salt]   **[Mold Blown Opaque Glass]**
            CIRCA: 1898 - 1905

A very unusual pattern design, reminiscent of a bark-like tree trunk containing 8 apricots. E. G. Warman called this pattern "Eight Ball Salt". The shaker is 2 3/4 inches tall. Observed only in the white-opaque glass.

2. ASTER   **[Mold Blown Opaque Glass]**
            CIRCA: 1892 - 1902
A four-sided shaker, 2½ inches tall, containing a large Aster upon each panel. Observed in white, blue and pink opaque glass. SCARCE

3. BARREL, FLORAL [NA]   **[Mold Blown Opaque Opalware]**
            CIRCA: 1888 - 1894
A satinized opalware shaker, 2½ inches tall, containing hand applied enamel floral decoration, similiar to the type of decorative practices of Mt. Washington Glass Co. Each shaker was no doubt individually decorated, and a matched pair would be a rare find.

4. BARREL, FLOWER BAND   **[Mold Blown Opaque Glass]**
            CIRCA: 1895 - 1905
As the pattern name implies, the principal motif consists of a floral band over 48 fine vertical ribs. This shaker measures 3¼ inches tall. Obsersved in white and blue opaque glass. SCARCE

1

2

3

4

PLATE XXXII

POTPOURRI

1. BARREL, TAPERED [NA] [Mold Blown Opaque Glass]
CIRCA: 1900 - 1908

Consisting of hand decorated opalware, 2½ inches tall, we have seen several over the last decade. As a motif, the outside is completely smooth, with a fired on solid tan coloring that contains various types and sizes of brown leaves. The artistic work is somewhat crude. Because the decoration is free hand-drawn, it is doubtful that an exact matched pair will be found.

2. BASKET, ROPE [NA] [Mold Blown & Pressed Glass]
CIRCA: 1906 - 1911

During this era several glass houses produced salt shakers that were made of opalware, and then painted in various solid colors. The item we have illustrated contains a tin top with a celluloid center and measures 2 5/8 inches tall. The motif resembles a basket with a rope tied around it. SCARCE

4. BEADED HEART [Mold Blown and Pressed Glass]
CIRCA: 1897 - 1907

With a height of 3½ inches, the pattern name fits the motif, which consists of six beaded hearts below six curving columns. When observed from the bottom, it appears to have a hexagon shape.

4. BILIKEN [Mold Blown and Pressed Glass]

This item was patented on October 6, 1908, as a "design for an image", by Florence Pretz of Kansas City, Mo. She was awarded patent No. 39603. As a collectible, it is sought after by bottle, glass and salt shaker collectors. Around the base is impressed: "The God of Things As They Ought To Be". This item has been made in crystal and milk-white glass. Our specimen has been painted with gilt. SCARCE

1

2

3

4

PLATE XXXIII

POTPOURRI

1. BIRD, CARNIVAL [NA]   **[Mold Blown and Pressed Glass]**
                             CIRCA: 1912 - 1920

Configured in the form of a bird, possibly a Robin, the body is of Rubigold Carnival Glass, the head is silver plated, with a small glass eye affixed on each side. This item is 2 3/4 inches tall. VERY SCARCE

2. BOWTIE, LARGE [NA]   **[Mold Blown and Pressed Glass]**
                             CIRCA: 1896 - 1906

An opaque-footed shaker 3 3/8 inches tall, the motif is reminscent of a "Bowtie" decorated with a gold border. We have had no additional color experience with this pattern. SCARCE

JEFFERSON GLASS CO.,
FOLLANSBEE, WEST VIRGINIA

3. BULBOUS SOUVENIR [NA]   **[Mold Blown Opaque Glass]**
                           CIRCA: 1909-1913

Of the several shakers that we have seen during the last twenty years, all have consisted of souvenir custard glass. The illustrated shaker is a souvenir of Richardton, N.D., and contains a pictorial view of St. Mary's Abbey. The shaker measures 3 inches tall, and contains a short ringed base. SCARCE.

4. BULLDOG, STANDING EAR [NA]   **[Mold Blown Glass]**
                           CIRCA: 1925 - 1935

This shaker has an identical glass body to the "CAT", except that a silver plated head of a Bulldog has been substituted. Apprently the Bulldog was intended for the dispensing of pepper, since the holes are twice the size of the companion "CAT". Observed in crystal, pink and green.

1

2

3

ST. MARY'S ABBEY,
RICHARDTON · N.D.

4

PLATE XXXIV

POTPOURRI

1. CAMEO VARIANT [NA]   [English Cameo Art Glass]
CIRCA: 1885 - 1895

A high-quality, frosted, free-blown art glass containing amber colored leaves and gooseberries in a slightly raised relief. We also have an identical shaker, with the same motif in blue, that Arthur G. Peterson named "CAMEO". This bulbous-shaped ware has a height of 3¼ inches, and should be considered VERY SCARCE.

2. CAMPHOR, SPECKLED [NA]   [Mold Blown Semi-opaque Glass]
CIRCA: 1883 - 1895

This is the only shaker of this type that we have ever seen. Consisting of an acidized, rough finish, with random speckling as the primary motif, it has many times been referred to as "Camphor Glass". The overall height measures 2 1/8 inches. RARE

3. CAT [NA]   [Mold Blown Glass]
CIRCA: 1925 - 1935

Considered to be a companion to the "Bulldog, Standing Ear", this item was originally a candy container that was designed for dispensing salt once the candy had been consumed. Standing 1 3/4 inches tall, this item has been observed in cyrstal, green and pink. The metal head contains dispensing holes between the ears. SCARCE

DITHRIDGE & CO.,
PITTSBURGH, PENNSYLVANIA

4. CORN   [Mold Blown Opaque Glass
CIRCA: 1896-1903

Several sizes and colors have been reported in this unusual pattern. In custard, as illustrated, it has been our experience that collection is a challenge. Observed in white, custard and green opaque glass. VERY SCARCE.

PLATE XXXV

POTPOURRI

1. CORN WITH HUSK [Mold Blown Opaque Glass]
CIRCA: 1899 - 1910

This ware was produced in several colors. All that we have seen contain a tin outer rim with a perforated celluloid center as a top. This shaker should not be confused with the so-called "Maize" ware produced by Libbey Glass during the late 1880 to early 1890 period. Our illustrated shaker measures 3 inches tall. SCARCE

2. CREASED NECK [Mold Blown Opaque Glass]
CIRCA: 1892 - 1898

Standing 3½ inches tall, most of these shakers were made by the Mt. Washington and Pairpoint glass houses. Over the years, we have acquired about twelve in our collection; all containing various types of floral decorations. An identically decorated pair should be considered VERY SCARCE.

3. CREASED WAIST, RIBBED [NA] [Mold Blown Opaque Glass]
CIRCA: 1898 - 1910

As the pattern name implies, the motif is a creased waist at the center separating melon type ribbing, with small individual scrolls around a bulging base. It has a height of 2 3/4 inches. No color has come to our attention. SCARCE

4. DAISY LONG PETAL [Mold Blown Opaque Glass]
CIRCA: 1904 - 1906

This ware was made by the "Consolidated Lamp and Glass Company of Pittsburgh and Coraopolis, Pa". Due to an oversight, we failed to include this item within the section of this book that attributes the shakers by Glass Houses. This is a difficult pattern to collect today, and apparently made only in a limited number of items. The shakers measure 3 3/8 inches tall. RARE

1

2

3

4

PLATE XXXVI

POTPOURRI

1. DAISY AND BUTTON SLENDER [Pressed Glass]
CIRCA: 1885 - 1892

This complete set, with companion stand, as illustrated is quite unique. The Daisy and Button pattern is repeated on top of the glass base, but the sides are plain. A protruding glass peg on each end of the stand fits into a hole in the bottom of each shaker. Known colors are crystal, blue, canary and amber. SCARCE

PAIRPOINT GLASS CO., NEW BEDFORD, MASSACHUSETTS

2. DAISY SPRIG [NA] [Mold Blown Opaque Glass]
CIRCA: 1896-1902

A satin glass shaker, 3 inches tall, with a peach-to-white shading, containing six individual hand-painted daisy sprigs as the motif. VERY SCARCE.

PAIRPOINT GLASS CO., NEW BEDFORD, MASSACHUSETTS

3. DAISY SPRIG VARIANT [NA] [Mold Blown Opaque Glass]
CIRCA: 1896-1902

This ware contains identical peach-to-white shading as described in the "Daisy Sprig" pattern. It is an obvious product of the same glass house. With a physical size of 2½ inches in diameter, the motif contains four hand-painted floral daisy springs. VERY SCARCE.

4. DIAMOND BLOCK VARIANT [NA] [Pressed Glass]
CIRCA: 1877 - 1884

An early pattern produced by several glass houses, which makes positive attribution essentially impossible. The shaker is 2 3/4 inches tall. Observed in crystal, amber and green. Known to have been produced in other colors. We recommend caution, since reproductions exist. SCARCE

PLATE XXXVII

POTPOURRI

1. DIAMOND POINT AND LEAF   [Mold Blown Opaque Glass]
CIRCA: 1893 - 1901
This pattern appears to have had limited production, primarily in novelty type items. In fact, we have only seen the salt and pepper shakers. Our color experience has amounted to crystal, opaque-white and opaque-blue. RARE

2. DIMINISHING SCROLLS [NA]   [Mold Blown Opaque Glass]
CIRCA: 1905 - 1912
This shaker is 2 3/4 inches tall. Encircling the bulging base are four diminishing scrolls which are repeated three times. The neck contains 18 vertical ribs. We have no color experience to report.

3. DISTENDED SIDES   [Mold Blown Opaque Glass]
CIRCA: 1902 - 1912
This ware appears to have been a part of a condiment set. Location of the complete set will be quite an acquisition. With a height of 2 3/8 inches, the motif consists of a single, large hand-painted floral spray. SCARCE

4. DOG   [Mold Blown Glass]
CIRCA: 1930 - 1940
This condiment dispenser appears to be a product from the so-called "Depression Era". The motif depicts a large-eared hound dog setting upon his haunches. Standing 3 3/4 inches tall, this item appears to have been a candy container that was devised for subsequent use as a salt shaker. Observed in crystal, amber and cobalt-blue. Reproductions of this item exist and the collector should exercise caution. In cobalt-blue the Dog is SCARCE.

PLATE XXXVIII

POTPOURRI

1. DOG, STANDING EAR [NA]   [Mold Blown Glass]
CIRCA: 1910 - 1020
A 2 1/8 inch tall, green cased-glass dog, with a metal head, reclining upon his haunches. Condiment is dispensed through perforated holes on the top of the head. We have no color experience to report. SCARCE

2. DOMINO   [Mold Blown Opaque Glass]
CIRCA: 1888 - 1898
We have been unable to definitely attribute this unusual shaker. Our best guess is W. L. Libbey & Sons of Toledo, Ohio. Configured in the image of four dominos molded together, some collectors refer to it as "double dice", or "pair of dice", which are incorrect names. This item is 3 1/8 inches tall. Made only in white opaque with intaglio black dots. VERY SCARCE

C.F. MONROE CO.,
MERIDEN, CONNECTICUT

3. DRAPED COLUMN [NA]   [Mold Blown Opaque Opalware]
CIRCA: 1900-1901
This is a very ornate opalware shaker 2 7/8 inches tall by 2½ inches in diameter. The motif resembles a group of tall draped columns above a bulging base. The latter contains a single floral decoration. SCARCE. From opalware blanks furnished by Pairpoint Glass Co. and then subsequently decorated by C.F. Monroe.

4. ELEPHANT   [Mold Blown Glass]
CIRCA: 1913 - 1922
We have two versions of this shaker. The glass body is identical, with the difference being in the shape of the trunk, which is a part of the metal top. It is also of interest to note that this same glass body can be found containing a metal top in the form of a monkey. In all cases, the glass body measures 2¼ inches tall. We have only observed this ware in crystal. VERY SCARCE

1

2

3

4

PLATE XXXIX

POTPOURRI

DITHRIDGE & CO., PITTSBURGH, PENNSYLVANIA

1. ERIE TWIST [Mold Blown Opaque Glass]
CIRCA: 1892-1905

A two inch tall shaker that was patented during October, 1892, by Carl V. Helmschmeid of Meriden, Connecticut. Collectors should exercise caution, because, the shakers have been reproduced in milkwhite glass. SCARCE. While this pattern was innovated (patented) by Carl Helmschmeid and marketed by C.F. Monroe, this particular pattern was produced by Dithridge for a number of years in various colored salt shakers. This same pattern was also produced for Monroe by Pairpoint in such configurations as pin boxes, lamps, etc.

2. FAN BASE [NA] [Mold Blown Glass]
CIRCA: 1905 - 1915

This is a relatively plain shaker, 2 7/8 inches tall. The motif consists of three intaglio fans around the base. Originally decorated with a light violet solid color that has suffered somewhat from the ravages of time.

3. FAN AND SCROLL [Mold Blown and Pressed Glass]
CIRCA: 1900 - 1910

This intricate pattern was named by Mr. E. G. Warman. The item is 2¼ inches tall, and 2 3/8 inches in diameter at the widest point. We have no color experience to report.

4. FATIMA SCROLL [Mold Blown Opaque Glass]
CIRCA: 1904 - 1910

Here is a 2¼ inch shaker containing a series of scrolls around the base, with six vertical vines, all in raised relief. We have had no color experience to report. SCARCE

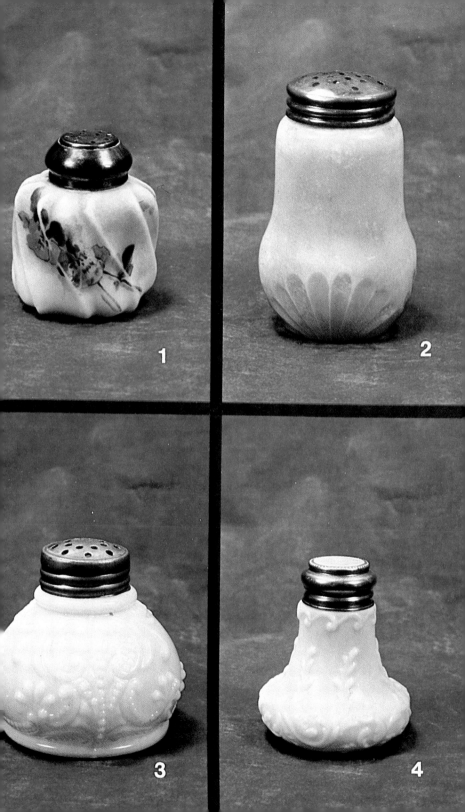

1

2

3

4

PLATE XXXX

POTPOURRI

1. FEATHER, LONG [NA]   [Mold Blown Opaque Glass]
CIRCA: 1898 - 1908
This ware represents one manufacturer's approach to the effects of salt corrosion problems. The top is made of one-piece threaded celluloid. This item is 2 7/8 inches tall with three long feathers in raised relief. Separating each feather is what appears to be a sprig of hand-painted orange poppies. SCARCE

2. FERN CONDIMENT [NA]   [Mold Blown and Pressed Opalware]
CIRCA: 1899 - 1908
This ware contains the salt, pepper and mustard, which fit within a scalloped opalware base measuring 5½ inches at the widest point. The shakers are 3¼ inches tall, and the mustard is 3 inches tall. The base shades from white at the bottom, to pink, at the top. The motif on each condiment dispenser consists of hand-painted brown ferns over a pink background. VERY SCARCE

3. FLEUR-DE-LIS BASE   [Mold Blown and Pressed Glass]
CIRCA: 1905 - 1915
A heavy opaque glass shaker, 3 1/16 inches tall, containing six fleur-de-lis spaced around six scalloped feet. Observed only in white opaque, some have painted floral designs.

4. FLEUR-DE-LIS WITH SCROLLING [NA]   [Mold Blown Custard Glass]
CIRCA: 1895 - 1905
The principal motif of this three mold shaker consists of three fleur-de-lis around the top and bottom, with intricate scrolling. It has an overall height of 2 3/8 inches. Observed in custard, blue and white opaque homogenous glass. VERY SCARCE

1

2

3

4

PLATE XXXXI

POTPOURRI

1. FLOWER WITH LEAVES [NA] [Mold Blown Opaque Glass]
CIRCA: 1902 - 1910
A short, bulging shaker, 2 inches tall by 3 1/8 inches in diameter. The motif consists of a large flower surrounded by seven leaves in raised-relief. The pattern is highlighted by the application of gilt paint.

2. FLOWER, SWIRL BEADED [NA] [Mold Blown & Pressed Glass]
CIRCA: 1905 - 1913
An unusual shaker, three inches tall, containing five large painted flowers interspersed between five beaded looping swirls. The two-piece top has a tin rim with a celluloid insert containing appropriate openings for dispensing salt and pepper. These celluloid centers were one of the several methods used by various manufacturers to avoid the corrosive action of the salt that was used during this era. SCARCE

3. FORGET ME-NOT TALL [Mold Blown Opaque Glass]
CIRCA: 1890 - 1900
Produced by Challinor, Taylor and Company after their merger with U.S. Glass Co. Really, a variation of Challinor's No. 20 (Forget-Me-Not) shown in Fig. 2 of Plate III. Made in various opaque colors (we have never seen it in crystal). A three panelled shaker containing small flowers within an intricate series of vines and leaves. Standing 2 3/4 inches tall, the observed colors are white, blue and green (all opaque). The illustrated shaker is VERY SCARCE.

4. GRECIAN GODDESS [NA] [Mold Blown & Pressed Glass]
CIRCA: 1925 - 1935
The bottom of this highly collectible item is marked "PAT 103910". It is an excellent example of a piece of glass that was marketed for dual usage. The lid, which is silver plated, contained a cardboard insert which, after removal revealed small holes through which a condiment (such as salt) might be dispensed. It is our opinion that it originally contained "cold cream". It stands 3 inches tall. Observed in white and black opaque. The black ones are SCARCE.

PLATE XXXXII

POTPOURRI

1. GRAPE SALT & PEPPER SET   [Mold Blown and Pressed Opalware]
CIRCA: 1903 - 1910

This is an unusual salt and pepper with companion tray. The salt shaker measures 2 5/8 inches tall; the pepper 2 ¼ inches tall; the tray is 5 3/8 inches long. Each piece contains a bunch of gilt-colored grapes and leaves. A complete set should be considered VERY SCARCE.

2. HYBRID VARIANT [NA]   [Mold Blown Glass]
CIRCA: 1875 - 1890

Consisting of a red ruby glass cylinder, the unusual metal framework slides over the upper part of the glass tube and clamps firmly in place by pressure from the screw-on scalloped top. One of our early acquisitions to the collection, it still remains a mysterious rarity. Observed colors are crystal and ruby. The glass cyclinder measures 3 3/8 inches tall. RARE

3. LEAF OVERLAPPING   [Mold Blown Opaque Glass]
CIRCA: 1896 - 1905

This is a 1 7/8 inch tall, squatty shaker that contains six rows of pointed leaves reminiscent of a type of thistle. Observed colors are white, blue, pink and green, all in opaque glass. Some can be found in cased glass. SCARCE

4. LEAF, SQUATTY [NA]   [Mold Blown and Pressed Glass]
CIRCA: 1902 - 1910

A bulging, squatty-based shaker, 3 inches in diameter and 2 inches tall, containing large leaves in raised relief curling upward from the bottom. We have no definite color experience to report. SCARCE

1

2

3

4

PLATE XXXXIII

POTPOURRI

I.J. STEANE & CO.,
HARTFORD, CONNECTICUT

1. LEAF, THREE [NA]   [Mold Blown Frosted Glass]
                    CIRCA: 1882-1891
This is a 2½ inch tall frosted glass shaker, with a two-piece pewter top that shades from a cobalt-blue at the bottom, to an electric-blue at the top. The principal motif consists of three hand-painted enamel leaves and white circular dots. This item appears to have been part of a condiment set. RARE. Marketed by Barbour Bros. Co. (for I.J. Steane) of Hartford, Connecticut.

2. LEAF ON SWIRL   [Mold Blown Opaque Glass]
                    CIRCA: 1898 - 1909
The glass composition of this shaker is among the most unusual that we have ever seen. After considerable study, we decided that it closely resembles the color of putty. Standing 3¼ inches tall, the motif consists of nine swirls with large leaves in raised relief around the base. This pattern is a challenge to collect. We have no additional color experience to report. VERY SCARCE

3. LEANING   [Mold Blown Opaque Glass]
                    CIRCA: 1890 - 1900
It is our opinion that this unsual design was created by Nicholas Kopp Jr., but we are not certain of the glass house of manufacture. With a height of 3¼ inches, all the shakers we have seen are opaque. Observed in white, blue and pink. VERY SCARCE

HELMSCHMEID MANUFACTURING CO.,
MERIDEN, CONNECTICUT

4. LOBE, SMALL [NA]   [Mold Blown and Pressed Glass]
                    CIRCA: 1903-1905
A small, lobe-shaped shaker, two inches tall, the principal motif consists of a pink rose with small green leaves, repeated three times around the circumference. Shading from white at the bottom to a solid lavender at the top, the color decor is created by fired on colors. VERY SCARCE.

1

2

3

4

PLATE XXXXIV

POTPOURRI

1. MARSH FLOWER [NA]   [Mold Blown Opaque Glass]
CIRCA: 1894 - 1904

This shaker shades from a pale-pink at the bottom, to a lemon-yellow at the top. With a height of 3¼ inches, the motif is similar to "Iris", but at least two other patterns exist under this name. We have no additional color experience to report. RARE

2. MELON, BEADED [NA]   [Mold Blown Opaque Glass]
CIRCA: 1898 - 1907

A somewhat squatty, melon-shaped shaker, 2½ inches tall, containing six bulging panels, each separated by a vertical beaded column. Observed only in white and blue, but no doubt made in other colors.

3. NINE LEAF, BULGING [NA]   [Mold Blown Opaque Glass]
CIRCA: 1900 - 1910

In our opinion, the assigned name describes the pattern adquately. A small shaker, 2½ inches tall, it appears to have been part of a condiment set. The plain design of the base no doubt was conceived for insertion into a glass or metal frame. No color has been observed or reported.

4. OLYMPIC [NA]   [Pressed Glass]
CIRCA: 1932

A very collectible combination salt and pepper dispenser, containing an internal glass divider (one side for salt and the other for pepper) with a two-section top containing perforations over each condiment vault. The perforations are in a normal closed condition. To obtain either salt or pepper, one must push-in on a spring-loaded metal tab, which opens the appropriate holes for dispensing of the desired condiment. The words "1932 OLYMPIC GAMES LOS ANGELES CALIF." are printed on the shaker body in raised relief. VERY SCARCE

PLATE XXXXV

POTPOURRI

1. OWL, BULGING [NA]   [Mold Blown Glass]
CIRCA: 1930 - 1940

The body is of crystal and the metal top is an owl head containing amber glass eyes. Completely assembled, the shaker resembles a bulging owl. The threaded glass body measures 2½ inches tall. VERY SCARCE

2. PIG IN A POKE [NA]   [Quality Porcelain]
CIRCA: 1890 - 1899

We like to call this cutie a conversation shaker. It was manufactured in Germany during the late 19th Century. The workmanship and detail are outstanding. This same pig was produced in a series of various poses. A find of this kind, although not of glass, should not be ignored, because it adds depth and value to a collection. RARE

3. PIG, STANDING [NA]   [Mold Blown Glass]
CIRCA: 1930 - 1940

Standing 2 inches tall, the body is of crystal and the head of amber-threaded glass. This is another candy container that was designed for subsequent use as a salt shaker. Observed also in solid crystal. SCARCE

4. PILLAR, TALL [NA]   [Mold Blown Opaque Glass]
CIRCA: 1885 - 1890

Here is a 3 1/8 inch tall, opaque, satin glass shaker containing a single hand-painted flower on a long green vine. It is a late addition to our collection, and was acquired too late for inclusion within the section of this book that contains manufacturer attribution. This item should be attributed to the MT. WASHINGTON GLASS CO., of New Bedford, Massachusetts. The quality of the glass is outstanding; the two piece metal top is of pewter. RARE

1

2

3

4

PLATE XXXXVI

POTPOURRI

1. PINEAPPLE FIGURE [Mold Blown Cased Glass]
CIRCA: 1891 - 1896
We had a little trouble accepting this pattern name which was established by a previous author, but will not add to the confusion by renaming it. This shaker is 3¼ inches tall, and stands upon four small feet which are surrounded by a series of plumes in raised relief. Observed colors are crystal, white, pink and blue. VERY SCARCE

MT. WASHINGTON GLASS CO.,
NEW BEDFORD, MASSACHUSETTS

2. RAFTER PANEL [Mold Blown Opaque Glass]
CIRCA: 1891-1894
An eight panelled shaker standing upon a circular base, the latter in raised relief. The principal motif is a large pair of painted leaves. This item measures 2½ inches tall. Observed only in white opaque with various painted flowers or leaves, some are made of satin glass. SCARCE.

3. RAINBOW BULBOUS [NA] [Free Blown Opaque Glass]
CIRCA: 1920 - 1930
A three inch tall shaker that appears to be of European origin, and in our opinion Venetian. So many people have admired and remarked on its beauty, that we have selected it for the cover of this book. It consists of multicolored vertical ribbons of glass with a thin, white inner-lining. This type of ware had a limited production, and was sold to the "Carraige Trade". The motif and craftsmanship are outstanding. RARE

4. REFRIGERATOR [Mold Blown and Pressed Glass]
CIRCA: 1925 - 1935
This unusual ware is configured in the form of the early General Electric type refrigerator. Some of the shakers contained a black-gummed paper label with the letters"GE" on it, and it was affixed to the door. It is of interest to note that matching sugar bowl was also produced. The salt shakers are 2 7/8 inches tall; the sugar bowl 3 5/8 inches tall. Shakers containing the original paper "GE" label are VERY SCARCE.

1

2

3

4

PLATE XXXXVII

POTPOURRI

1. RIB ALTERNATING [Mold Blown Cased Glass]
CIRCA: 1897 - 1903

A wide-based shaker containing eight large ribs, this item stands 3 1/8 inches tall. The unique brass top is original, and equipped with a knurled outer ring for opening and closing the condiment dispensing holes. Colors observed are white, pink, green and blue. SCARCE

2. RIBBED [Mold Blown Opaque Glass]
CIRCA: 1897 - 1906

A relatively small shaker, 2 5/8 inches tall, the lower-half contains 36 vertical beaded ribs. The upper part, above a beaded ring, is decorated with a floral spray applied over a light-tan background.

3. RIB, BULBOUS TWENTY-FOUR [NA] [Mold Blown Opaque Glass]
CIRCA: 1890 - 1900

A bulbous shaped shaker 2½ inches tall, containing 24 vertical ribs, this ware was manufactured in opaque homogenous colors. It has not been observed in crystal. SCARCE

4. RIB, SQUATTY [NA] [Mold Blown Opaque Glass]
CIRCA: 1905 - 1915

A somewhat delicate, thin glass, 2½ inches tall, this shaker contains a gilt colored band in relief above nine wide ribs. Each rib is separated by a column of four beads. We have had no color experience to report. SCARCE

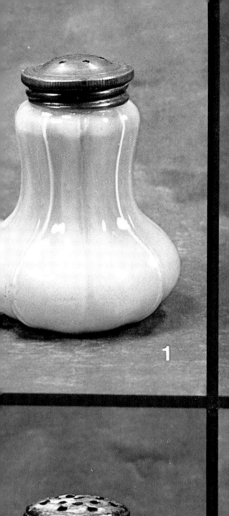

PLATE XXXXVIII

POTPOURRI

1. RIB AND SWIRL [Mold Blown Opaque Glass]
CIRCA: 1875 - 1885

This is one of the larger shakers in our collection standing 4 1/8 inches tall. We have studied the glass composition and find it to be an exact match with the early milk-white glass contained in our "Johnny Bull" saloon pepper produced by Atterbury and Co., of Pittsburgh, Pa., during the 1870 period. The base contains 27 short vertical ribs and a swirl pattern at the top.VERY SCARCE

2. RIB, TWELVE PANEL [NA] [Mold Blown Opaque Glass]
CIRCA: 1904 - 1912

This salt measures 3 5/8 inches tall. The motif consists of twelve ribbed panels, containing hand-painted leaf and flower decorations. Our color experience is limited to the shaker we are illustrating. SCARCE

3. SCROLL, BEADED [NA] [Mold Blown Opaque Glass]
CIRCA: 1904 - 1910

A 3¼ inch tall shaker, the motif consists of a series of fine beads enclosed within a fancy scrolled framework. This pattern is repeated, with even spacing, three times. We have only observed this shaker in white-opaque. SCARCE

CONSOLIDATED LAMP & GLASS CO., PITTSBURGH & CORAPOLIS, PENNSYLVANIA

4. SCROLL, FOOTED [Mold Blown Cased Glass]
CIRCA: 1895-1901

A square-based shaker, 3¼ inches tall, this item has four small glass feet. Each of the four panels contain an intricate scroll design. Observed colors are crystal, white-opaque, blue and pink. The cased glass shakers are VERY SCARCE.

PLATE XXXXIX

POTPOURRI

1. SCROLL AND LEAF, HEXAGON [NA]　　　　[Mold Blown Glass]
CIRCA: 1897 - 1905

A three inch tall, hexagon shaker, this item has a different scroll and leafy motif on each panel in raised relief. The upper-part of every third panel also contains a small hand-painted floral spray. VERY SCARCE

2. SCROLL, LOW　　　　[Mold Blown Opaque Glass]
CIRCA: 1894 - 1902

A bulging-shaped shaker, 2 3/8 inches tall, this pattern contains six identically scrolled panels that rise from a hexagon-shaped base. Our color experience has amounted to white, pink and green, all in opaque glass. SCARCE

3. SCROLL, NARROW BASED　　　　[Mold Blown Opaque Glass]
CIRCA: 1894 - 1901

Here is a 3 5/8 inch tall, four sided shaker. The motif consists of a large complex scroll in raised relief. This decoration is contained on two of the four panels; the other two are plain. Observed colors are white, blue, pale-green and pink, all in opaque. SCARCE

4. SCROLL WITH PANSIES [NA]　　　　[Mold Blown Opaque Glass]
CIRCA: 1902 - 1912

This ware was originally hand-painted, but time and usage have obliterated the original color scheme. As the pattern name implies, the motif consists of two pansies within an intricate scrolling design repeated two times. The shaker is 3 3/8 inches tall. SCARCE

PLATE XXXXX

POTPOURRI

1. SUGAR AND CREAMER, MINIATURE [NA]   [Pressed Glass]
CIRCA: 1910 - 1920

An unusual pair of condiment dispensers, 1½ inches tall, they are configured in the form of a miniature sugar and creamer. Their glass bases are identical and interchangeable. They are probably a product of an American Silver Company, since the identify of each shaker is formed by each respective silver-plated metal top. VERY SCARCE

2. SWIRL AND FERN OPALESCENT [NA]   [Mold Blown and Pressed Glass]
CIRCA: 1925 - 1935

This is a relatively late shaker, 3 3/8 inches tall, containing eight white-opalescent, fern-like, swirling leaves. A similar motif was also manufactured for use as a cologne dispenser.

3. SWIRL, LARGE [NA]   [Mold Blown and Pressed Glass]
CIRCA: 1900 - 1910

A large, heavy shaker, 4 1/8 inches tall, the motif consists of nine large swirls with an octagon base. We have observed it only in white-opaque, but other colors no doubt were made. SCARCE

4. THOUSAND EYE, RINGED CENTER   [Pressed Glass]
CIRCA: 1875 - 1882

A rare pattern. All that we have ever seen is the shakers. If this pattern was made in other pieces, we have not been able to confirm same. The shakers measure 3 1/8 inches tall. Observed colors are crystal, canary, amber, blue, and green. RARE

1

2

3

4

PLATE XXXXXI

POTPOURRI

1. THUMBPRINT, BABY SMALL [NA]   [Mold Blown Glass]
CIRCA: 1880 - 1890

This is another example of the expensive dual-mold process in a lovely cranberry color. A small shaker, 2 inches tall, containing a two-piece pewter top, the motif is a baby thumbprint on the inside, and completely smooth on the outside. It is made in a variety of colors by many glass houses, attribution is amost impossible. The collector should exercise caution, because excellent reproductions of this pattern have been coming out of Europe for the last decade. VERY SCARCE

2. THUMBPRINT, CONCAVE FOOTED [NA]   [Mold Blown Glass]
CIRCA: 1910 - 1920

This shaker was formed by the dual-mold process. The outer-body is completely smooth. The inside contains a diamond concave thumbprint pattern. The color is a deep ruby-red, shading to a amberina color which can be clearly seen by removing the metal top. This item measures 3 3/8 inches tall. RARE

3. VINE, THREE FOOT [NA]   [Mold Blown Opaque Glass]
CIRCA: 1898 - 1906

This pattern consists of an intricate vine that is repeated three times. A beaded ring encircles the shaker just below the metal top. The height is 2½ inches, and is supported upon three small feet. We have no color experience to report on this item. SCARCE

4. VIOLET SPRIG CONDIMENT [NA]   [Mold Blown & Pressed Glass]
CIRCA: 1897 - 1905

This is a delicate, almost impractically designed, condiment set. The glass base reminds one of three individual half-eggs molded together and drilled in the center for placement of the metal lifting handle. Each condiment dispenser fits within the aforementioned openings. The survival factor of the base was obviously very poor. Each individual shaker and mustard measured 2¼ inches tall, and are decorated with a hand-painted violet floral spring. VERY SCARCE

PLATE XXXXXII

POTPOURRI

1. WAIST BAND [Mold Blown Opaque Glass]
CIRCA: 1894 - 1900

Standing 3 3/4 inches, this is a relatively tall salt. A band of four rings divide the upper and lower ribbing at the center. Observed in white, blue, pink and custard. The custard shakers are RARE.

PAIRPOINT GLASS CO.,
NEW BEDFORD, MASSACHUSETTS

2. WREATH, TWELVE PANEL [NA] [Mold Blown Opaque Glass]
CIRCA: 1895-1900

The motif consists of a twelve panelled shaker, 2 7/8 inches tall, with two large floral wreaths between scrolls near the top edge, and a scalloped bottom. Each floral wreath is separated by a small flower spray. VERY SCARCE.

3. ZIGZAG [Mold Blown and Pressed Opaque Glass]
CIRCA: 1902 - 1906

This ware was marketed as a condiment set containing salt, pepper and mustard. The shakers are 3 inches tall with a motif that resembles six expanded Z's equally spaced. It has been observed only in white-opaque. A complete set should be considered VERY SCARCE.

SALT SHAKER VALUES VS SCARCITY

The retail values listed below are intended to serve as a GUIDE to the collector, dealer for the shakers illustrated in this book. We have offered a value spread which allows for consideration of the condition of each item. If in mint condition, the higher suggested value should be considered. If you are fortunate enough to locate a shaker priced well below our recommended minimum, you will probably have located a so-called "Sleeper", assuming no reproduction.

The scarcity factors assigned to the various categories of shakers are based upon over twenty years of specialized salt shaker collection experience. Our judgment are based upon our visitation to hundreds (perhaps thousands) of antique shops shows attended, flea markets, junk shops, etc., in all parts of the Country. In addition, we have maintained a continuous value file, taken from the major periodical publications, involving hundreds of mail order dealers. This data has been utilized in preparing our current value guidelines.

Many of the circumstances and decisions associated with collecting this ware are of a judgmental nature. Most decisions must be made upon the basis of personal experience and knowledge. The asking price of an item can hardly be adjudicated if the scarcity of an item is unknown. While it is recognized that such factors as collectibility, type and quality of the glass, etc., also determine price scarcity comprises the main determinate that most dealers appear to use in evaluating price. We have tried to consider all of the above factors in establishing our recommended values.

It should be noted that many of the old shakers that contain glass threading, will have visible flaking when the top is removed. This should not form the basis for considering the item to be in damaged condition. Practically all mold-blown shakers were taken off the pontil rod at the top; the glass houses left them as-is because this roughness and chipping is hidden by the metal top.

The collecting of art glass shakers such as New England Peachblow, Holly Amber, Burmese, Webb Peachblow, Agata, Pomona, Amberina, Wheeling Peachblow Tiffany, Steuben, etc., are difficult. When located, the cost will usually be high and you will be faced with the dilemma of how much to pay, and whether to purchase or not. This type of ware has a high scarcity factor, and the only advice that can be offered is to recommend that a few art glass shakers be acquired in order to add value and depth to a collection.

PLATE I

Fig. 1.	Johnny Bull	Single	$	95.00-	115.00
		Pair	$	175.00-	200.00
Fig. 2.	Owl, Little	Single	$	125.00-	140.00
Fig. 3.	Barrel, Christmas	Single	$	70.00-	85.00
	Without Agitator	Single	$	38.00-	47.00
Fig. 4.	Lafayet Salt Boat	Museum Piece		Not	Valued

PLATE II

Fig. 1.	Atlas	Single	$	22.00-	30.00
		Pair	$	33.00-	41.00
Fig. 2.	Beehive	Single	$	26.00-	34.00
		Pair	$	35.00-	45.00
Fig. 3.	Opal-Ribbon, Short	Single	$	38.00-	46.00
		Pair	$	62.00-	75.00
Fig. 4.	Chrysanthemum Base	Single	$	41.00-	50.00
		Pair	$	70.00-	85.00

PLATE III

Fig. 1.	Star of Bethlehem	Single	$	26.00-	35.00
		Pair	$	36.00-	48.00
Fig. 2.	Challinor's No. 20	Single	$	30.00-	36.00
		Pair	$	42.00-	51.00
	Complete Set w/matching cruet & tray	Complete	$	155.00-	175.00
Fig. 3.	Bulging Three Petal Condiment	Complete	$	210.00-	230.00

PLATE IV

Fig. 1.	Bulging Leaf	Single	$	28.00-	35.00
		Pair	$	40.00-	55.00
Fig. 2.	Half Cone	Single	$	62.00-	70.00
		Pair	$	80.00-	97.00
Fig. 3.	Cotton Bale	Single	$	29.00-	36.00
		Pair	$	45.00-	56.00
Fig. 4.	Cone	Single	$	24.00-	30.00
		Pair	$	37.00-	48.00

PLATE V

Fig. 1.	Flower Assortment	Single	$	35.00-	45.00
		Pair	$	55.00-	70.00
Fig. 2.	Guttate	Single	$	36.00-	47.00
		Pair	$	60.00-	75.00
Fig. 3.	Guttate, Squatty	Single	$	45.00-	58.00
		Pair	$	77.00-	89.00
Fig. 4.	Shell, Overlapping	Single	$	30.00-	36.00
		Pair	$	45.00-	58.00

PLATE VI

Fig. 1.	Bulge Bottom	Single	$	40.00-	52.00
		Pair	$	55.00-	70.00
Fig. 2.	Creased Bale	Single	$	50.00-	62.00
		Pair	$	77.00-	90.00
	Complete Condiment	Complete	$	190.00-	210.00
Fig. 3.	Heart	Single	$	50.00-	60.00
		Pair	$	75.00-	90.00
Fig. 4.	Scroll and Square	Single	$	31.00-	39.00
		Pair	$	47.00-	57.00

PLATE VII

Fig. 1. Spider Web	Single $	34.00-	41.00
	Pair $	45.00-	59.00
Fig. 2. Sunset	Single $	35.00-	42.00
	Pair $	47.00-	65.00
Fig. 3. Swirl Diagonal Wide	Single $	36.00-	45.00
	Pair $	50.00-	63.00
Fig. 4. Teardrop, Bulging	Single $	24.00-	33.00
	Pair $	37.00-	55.00

PLATE VIII

Fig. 1. Torch and Wreath	Single $	40.00-	50.00
	Pair $	65.00-	77.00
Fig. 2. Shell and Tassel	Single $	45.00-	56.00
	Pair $	70.00-	85.00
Fig. 3. Button Arches	Single $	28.00-	39.00
	Pair $	46.00-	57.00
Fig. 4. Butterfly	Single $	31.00-	43.00
	Pair $	58.00-	69.00

PLATE IX

Fig. 1. Cosmos Scroll Condiment	Single $	22.00-	30.00
	Pair $	41.00-	53.00
Complete with glass tray	$	130.00-	155.00
Fig. 2. Fleur-de-lis Condiment	Single $	20.00-	27.00
	Pair $	33.00-	41.00
Complete with glass tray	$	55.00-	65.00
Fig. 3. Flower Blooming	Single $	33.00-	40.00
	Pair $	45.00-	55.00
Fig. 4. Forget-me-not-peewee and Companion	Single $	20.00-	25.00
	Pair $	32.00-	40.00
Complete with glass tray	$	78.00-	90.00

PLATE X

Fig. 1. Tulip Base	Single $	27.00-	34.00
	Pair $	46.00-	58.00
Fig. 2. Melon	Single $	35.00-	42.00
	Pair $	65.00-	78.00
Muffineer (Sugar Shaker)	$	160.00-	190.00
Fig. 3. Diamond & Star	Single $	30.00-	40.00
	Pair $	51.00-	65.00
Fig. 4. Diamond & Zipper	Single $	28.00-	36.00
	Pair $	49.00-	61.00

PLATE XI

Fig. 1. Ivorina Verde	Single $	65.00-	76.00
	Pair $	100.00-	115.00
Fig. 2. Punty Band	Single $	60.00-	72.00
	Pair $	85.00-	97.00

PLATE XII

Fig. 1. Acorn	Single	$	47.00-	55.00
	Pair	$	70.00-	85.00
Fig. 2. Pillar, Sixteen	Single	$	56.00-	63.00
	Pair	$	85.00-	99.00
Fig. 3. Swirl, Opalescent	Single	$	65.00-	72.00
	Pair	$	90.00-	105.00
Fig. 4. Thumbprint Inverted Round	Single	$	45.00-	51.00
	Pair	$	68.00-	80.00

PLATE XIII

Fig. 1. Grape, Carnival	Pair	$	15.00-	22.50
Fig. 2. Johnny Bull (Carnival)	Pair	$	21.00-	30.00
Fig. 3. Mary Bull	Pair	$	17.00-	24.00
Fig. 4. Sphinx	Single	$	65.00-	75.00
	Pair	$	100.00-	115.00

PLATE XIV

Fig. 1. Hybrid (Solid Metal Tube)	Single	$	12.00-	18.00
	Pair	$	24.00-	31.00
Fig. 2. Hybrid (Open Scrolled)	Single	$	23.00-	28.00
	Pair	$	32.00-	39.00
Fig. 3. Same as Fig. 2			-----------------	
Fig. 4. Hybrid (Bulbous Shaped)	Single	$	35.00-	40.00
	Pair	$	41.00-	50.00

PLATE XV

Fig. 1. Circle Double	Single	$	55.00-	67.00
	Pair	$	85.00-	94.00
Fig. 2. Iris	Single	$	31.00-	37.00
	Pair	$	42.00-	55.00
Fig. 3. Ribbed Thumbprint	Single	$	21.00-	26.00
	Pair	$	29.00-	40.00
Fig. 4. Swag With Brackets	Single	$	60.00-	70.00
	Pair	$	80.00-	95.00

PLATE XVI

Fig. 1. Lalique Intaglio	Single	$	70.00-	77.00
	Pair	$	90.00-	105.00
Fig. 2. Dice	Single	$	110.00-	125.00
	Pair	$	145.00-	158.00

PLATE XVII

Fig. 1. Intaglio Swirl	Single	$	28.00-	35.00
	Pair	$	35.00-	42.00
Fig. 2. Flower Panel	Single	$	16.00-	24.00
	Pair	$	30.00-	37.00
Fig. 3. Scrolled Neck with Plume	Single	$	18.00-	21.00
	Pair	$	26.00-	40.00
Fig. 4. Colonial, English	Single	$	14.00-	20.00
	Pair	$	26.00-	35.00

PLATE XVIII

Fig. 1. Meissen	Single	$	45.00-	58.00
	Pair	$	65.00-	75.00
Complete Condiment		$	100.00-	115.00
Fig. 2. Scroll, Wave	Single	$	75.00-	90.00
	Pair	$	125.00-	138.00

PLATE XIX

Fig. 1. Crown Milano	Single	$ 65.00-	78.00
	Pair	$ 110.00-	125.00
Fig. 2. Egg, Flat End	Single	$ 75.00-	82.00
	Pair	$ 110.00-	120.00
Fig. 3. Egg, Flat Side	Single	$ 65.00-	78.00
	Pair	$ 100.00-	125.00
Fig. 4. Pillar, Ribbed	Single	$ 55.00-	62.00
	Pair	$ 80.00-	90.00

PLATE XX

Fig. 1. Floral Spray	Single	$ 65.00-	78.00
	Pair	$ 90.00-	105.00
Fig. 2. Lobe, Five	Single	$ 47.00-	60.00
	Pair	$ 68.00-	85.00
Fig. 3. Scroll and Bulge	Single	$ 50.00-	60.00
	Pair	$ 67.00-	78.00
Fig. 4. Two Flower Sprig	Single	$ 125.00-	135.00
	Pair	$ 210.00-	225.00

PLATE XXI

Fig. 1. Egg, Flat End Variant	Single	$ 130.00-	145.00
	Pair	$ 210.00-	235.00
Fig. 2. Fig	Single	$ 110.00-	122.00
	Matched pair	$ 275.00-	315.00
Fig. 3. Floral Dome	Single	$ 85.00-	97.00
	Pair	$ 115.00-	127.00
Fig. 4. Royal Flemish	Single	$ 250.00-	270.00
	Pair	$ 550.00-	610.00

PLATE XXII

Fig. 1. Leaf, Berry Four Feet	Single	$ 100.00-	112.00
	Pair	$ 145.00-	175.00
Fig. 2. Loop and Daisy	Single	$ 70.00-	80.00
	Pair	$ 105.00-	120.00
Fig. 3. Egg in Cup	Single	$ 95.00-	110.00
	Pair	$ 145.00-	170.00
Fig. 4. Lobe, Squatty	Single	$ 85.00-	96.00
	Pair	$ 115.00-	130.00

PLATE XXIII

Fig. 1. Tomato	Single, white	$ 47.00-	55.00
	Single, shaded colors	$ 65.00-	80.00
Undeveloped Burmese	Single	$ 130.00-	150.00
Undeveloped Burmese	Pair	$ 200.00-	225.00
Fig. 2. Tomato, Large (muffineer)	Single	$ 275.00-	300.00
Fig. 3. Bird Arbor	Single	$ 105.00-	120.00
	Pair	$ 145.00-	165.00
Fig. 4. Lobe, Six	Single	$ 90.00-	100.00
	Pair	$ 115.00-	128.00

PLATE XXIV

Fig. 1. Orinda	Single	$	32.00-	40.00
	Pair	$	48.00-	60.00
Fig. 2. S. Repeat	Single Amethyst	$	67.00-	75.00
	Pair Amethyst	$	88.00-	97.00
Fig. 3. Curved Body	Single	$	25.00-	33.00
	Pair	$	45.00-	55.00
Fig. 4. Many Petals	Single	$	35.00-	42.00
	Pair	$	47.00-	58.00

PLATE XXV

Fig. 1. Blossomtime Variant	Single	$	115.00-	128.00
	Pair	$	230.00-	250.00
Fig. 2. Mother-of-Pearl Raindrop	Single	$	150.00-	165.00
	Pair	$	250.00-	275.00
Fig. 3. New England Peachblow	Single	$	550.00-	590.00
	Pair	$1,100.00-1,250.00			
Fig. 4. Rubina	Single	$	110.00-	125.00
	Pair	$	130.00-	145.00

PLATE XXVI

Fig. 1. Chrysanthemum Sprig	Single	$	110.00-	128.00
	Pair	$	132.00-	139.00
Fig. 2. Alaska	Single	$	65.00-	77.00
	Pair	$	80.00-	95.00
Fig. 3. Alaska Variant	Single	$	65.00-	77.00
	Pair	$	80.00-	95.00
Fig. 4. Circled Scroll	Single	$	76.00-	85.00
	Pair	$	95.00-	115.00

PLATE XXVII

Fig. 1. Jewel and Flower	Single	$	70.00-	85.00
	Pair	$	97.00-	115.00
Fig. 2. Everglades	Single	$	80.00-	110.00
	Pair	$	130.00-	155.00
Fig. 3. Richmond	Single	$	20.00-	28.00
	Pair	$	31.00-	38.00
Fig. 4. Cornucopia	Single	$	33.00-	39.00
	Pair	$	42.00-	49.00

PLATE XXVIII

Fig. 1. Croesus	Single green	$	63.00-	72.00
	Pair green	$	79.00-	90.00
	Single, amethyst	$	85.00-	96.00
	Pair, amethyst	$	110.00-	125.00
Fig. 2. Empress	Single green	$	65.00-	78.00
	Pair green	$	85.00-	105.00
	Single amethyst	$	85.00-	96.00
	Pair amethyst	$	145.00-	160.00
Fig. 3. X-ray	Single	$	82.00-	95.00
	Pair	$	110.00-	120.00
Fig. 4. Longwy	Single	$	88.00-	99.00
	Pair	$	130.00-	145.00

PLATE XXXV

Fig. 1.	Corn With Husk .... Single	$	36.00-	42.00
	Pair	$	57.00-	60.00
Fig. 2.	Creased Neck .... Single	$	26.00-	34.00
	With two-piece pewter top .... Single	$	39.00-	51.00
	Matched pair, identical decoration .... Pair	$	90.00-	115.00
Fig. 3.	Creased Waist, Ribbed..................... Single	$	27.00-	38.00
	Pair	$	46.00-	60.00
Fig. 4.	Daisy Long Petal .... Single	$	64.00-	80.00
	Pair	$	95.00-	118.00

PLATE XXXVI

Fig. 1.	Daisy and Button Slender .... Single	$	21.00-	29.00
	Pair	$	37.00-	46.00
	Complete with Glass Base .... Complete	$	77.00-	91.00
Fig. 2.	Daisy Sprig .... Single	$	45.00-	55.00
	Pair	$	81.00-	96.00
Fig. 3.	Daisy Sprig Variant .... Single	$	48.00-	56.00
	Pair	$	88.00-	110.00
Fig. 4.	Diamond Block Variant..................... Single	$	34.00-	42.00
	Pair	$	55.00-	69.00

PLATE XXXVII

Fig. 1.	Diamond Point and Leaf.................... Single	$	58.00-	65.00
	Pair	$	97.00-	115.00
Fig. 2.	Diminishing Scrolls........................ Single	$	26.00-	34.00
	Pair	$	37.00-	43.00
Fig. 3.	Distended Sides........................... Single	$	18.00-	26.00
	Pair	$	31.00-	39.00
Fig. 4.	Dog..................................... Single	$	33.00-	49.00
	Pair	$	45.00-	59.00

PLATE XXXVIII

Fig. 1.	Dog, Standing Ear .... Single	$	55.00-	67.00
	Pair	$	75.00-	91.00
Fig. 2.	Domino .... Single	$	71.00-	82.00
	Pair	$	100.00-	125.00
Fig. 3.	Draped Column .... Single	$	48.00-	56.00
	Pair	$	65.00-	80.00
Fig. 4.	Elephant................................. Single	$	55.00-	61.00
	Pair	$	68.00-	85.00

PLATE XXXIX

Fig. 1.	Erie Twist............................... Single	$	90.00-	115.00
	Pair	$	135.00-	148.00
Fig. 2.	Fan Base................................ Single	$	16.00-	22.00
	Pair	$	21.00-	32.00
Fig. 3.	Fan and Scroll .... Single	$	26.00-	31.00
	Pair	$	37.00-	45.00
Fig. 4.	Fatima Scroll .... Single	$	19.00-	27.00
	Pair	$	31.00-	41.00

PLATE XL

Fig. 1. Feather, Long	Single	$	33.00-	37.0
	Pair	$	40.00-	50.0
Fig. 2. Fern, Condiment	Complete	$	105.00-	125.0
Fig. 3. Fleur-De-Lis Base	Single	$	23.00-	30.0
	Pair	$	35.00-	49.0
Fig. 4. Fleur-De-Lis With Scrolling	Single	$	49.00-	61.0
	Pair	$	85.00-	100.0

PLATE XLI

Fig. 1. Flower with Leaves	Single	$	15.00-	22.0
	Pair	$	28.00-	34.0
Fig. 2. Flower Swirl, Beaded	Single	$	20.00-	31.0
	Pair	$	39.00-	46.0
Fig. 3. Forget Me-Not, Tall	Single	$	37.00-	48.0
	Pair	$	55.00-	70.0
Fig. 4. Grecian Goddess	Single	$	34.00-	40.0
	Pair	$	46.00-	57.0

PLATE XLII

Fig. 1. Grape Salt & Pepper Set	Complete	$	65.00-	79.0
Fig. 2. Hybrid Variant	Single	$	56.00-	67.0
	Pair	$	85.00-	97.0
Fig. 3. Leaf Overlapping	Single	$	34.00-	42.0
	Pair	$	57.00-	70.0
Fig. 4. Leaf, Squatty	Single	$	19.00-	26.0
	Pair	$	29.00-	41.00

PLATE XLIII

Fig. 1. Leaf, Three	Single	$	68.00-	79.00
	Pair	$	97.00-	115.00
Fig. 2. Leaf On Swirl	Single	$	56.00-	63.0
	Pair	$	71.00-	82.00
Fig. 3. Leaning	Single	$	60.00-	70.0
	Pair	$	105.00-	127.00
Fig. 4. Lobe, Small	Single	$	23.00-	31.00
	Pair	$	36.00-	50.00

PLATE XLIV

Fig. 1. Marsh Flower	Single	$	40.00-	49.00
	Pair	$	58.00-	70.00
Fig. 2. Melon, Beaded	Single	$	18.00-	24.00
	Pair	$	31.00-	40.00
Fig. 3. Nine Leaf Bulging	Single	$	12.00-	19.00
	Pair	$	25.00-	35.00
Fig. 4. Olympic	Single	$	42.00-	49.00

PLATE XLV

Fig. 1. Owl, Bulging	Single	$	23.00-	31.00
	Pair	$	38.00-	45.00
Fig. 2. Pig In A Poke	Single	$	105.00-	130.00
	Pair	$	165.00-	180.00
Fig. 3. Pig, Standing	Single	$	25.00-	30.00
	Pair	$	35.00-	43.00
Fig. 4. Pillar, Tall	Single	$	81.00-	97.00
	Pair	$	115.00-	128.00

PLATE XLVI

Fig. 1.	Pineapple Figure	Single	$	45.00- 56.00
		Pair	$	61.00- 77.00
Fig. 2.	Rafter Panel	Single	$	36.00- 47.00
		Pair	$	53.00- 65.00
Fig. 3.	Rainbow Bulbous	Single	$	130.00- 140.00
		Pair	$	185.00- 200.00
Fig. 4.	Refrigerator	Single	$	27.00- 34.00
		Pair	$	42.00- 57.00
	With GE paper label	Single	$	35.00- 43.00
		Pair	$	55.00- 68.00

PLATE XLVII

Fig. 1.	Rib, Alternating	Single	$	29.00- 36.00
		Pair	$	46.00- 60.00
Fig. 2.	Ribbed	Single	$	21.00- 29.00
		Pair	$	25.00- 37.00
Fig. 3.	Rib, Bulbous Twenty-Four	Single	$	34.00- 40.00
		Pair	$	46.00- 55.00
Fig. 4.	Rib, Squatty	Single	$	26.00- 30.00
		Pair	$	36.00- 43.00

PLATE XLVIII

Fig. 1.	Rib and Swirl	Single	$	37.00- 45.00
		Pair	$	51.00- 59.00
Fig. 2.	Rib, Twelve Panel	Single	$	35.00- 40.00
		Pair	$	55.00- 65.00
Fig. 3.	Scroll, Beaded	Single	$	21.00- 29.00
		Pair	$	29.00- 37.00
Fig. 4.	Scroll, Footed	Single	$	45.00- 52.00
		Pair	$	56.00- 70.00

PLATE XLIX

Fig. 1.	Scroll and Leaf, Hexagon	Single	$	34.00- 38.00
		Pair	$	49.00- 60.00
Fig. 2.	Scroll, Low	Single	$	30.00- 40.00
		Pair	$	45.00- 55.00
Fig. 3.	Scroll, Narrow Based	Single	$	31.00- 42.00
		Pair	$	49.00- 61.00
Fig. 4.	Scroll with Pansies	Single	$	21.00- 28.00
		Pair	$	30.00- 36.00

PLATE L

Fig. 1.	Sugar and Creamer, Miniature	Pair	$	41.00- 60.00
Fig. 2.	Swirl and Fern Opalescent	Single	$	16.00- 22.00
		Pair	$	24.00- 30.00
Fig. 3.	Swirl, Large	Single	$	21.00- 32.00
		Pair	$	30.00- 37.00
Fig. 4.	Thousand Eye, Ringed Center	Single	$	31.00- 40.00
		Pair	$	68.00- 79.00

PLATE LI

Fig. 1. Thumbprint Baby, Small	Single $	46.00-	52.00
	Pair $	60.00-	75.00
Fig. 2. Thumbprint, Concave Footed	Single $	67.00-	74.00
	Pair $	115.00-	135.00
Fig. 3. Vine, Three Foot	Single $	25.00-	30.00
	Pair $	33.00-	39.00
Fig. 4. Violet Sprig Condiment	Complete $	110.00-	130.00

PLATE LII

Fig. 1. Waist Band	Single $	33.00-	45.00
	Pair $	45.00-	55.00
Fig. 2. Wreath, Twelve Panel	Single $	35.00-	45.00
	Pair $	56.00-	65.00
Fig. 3. Zigzag	Single $	29.00-	36.00
	Pair $	41.00-	50.00
Three piece condiment	Complete $	65.00-	77.00

* * * * * * * * * * * *

MASTER INDEX

The pattern name of each piece of glass in this book is listed in alphabetical order followed by the page number that it appears upon.